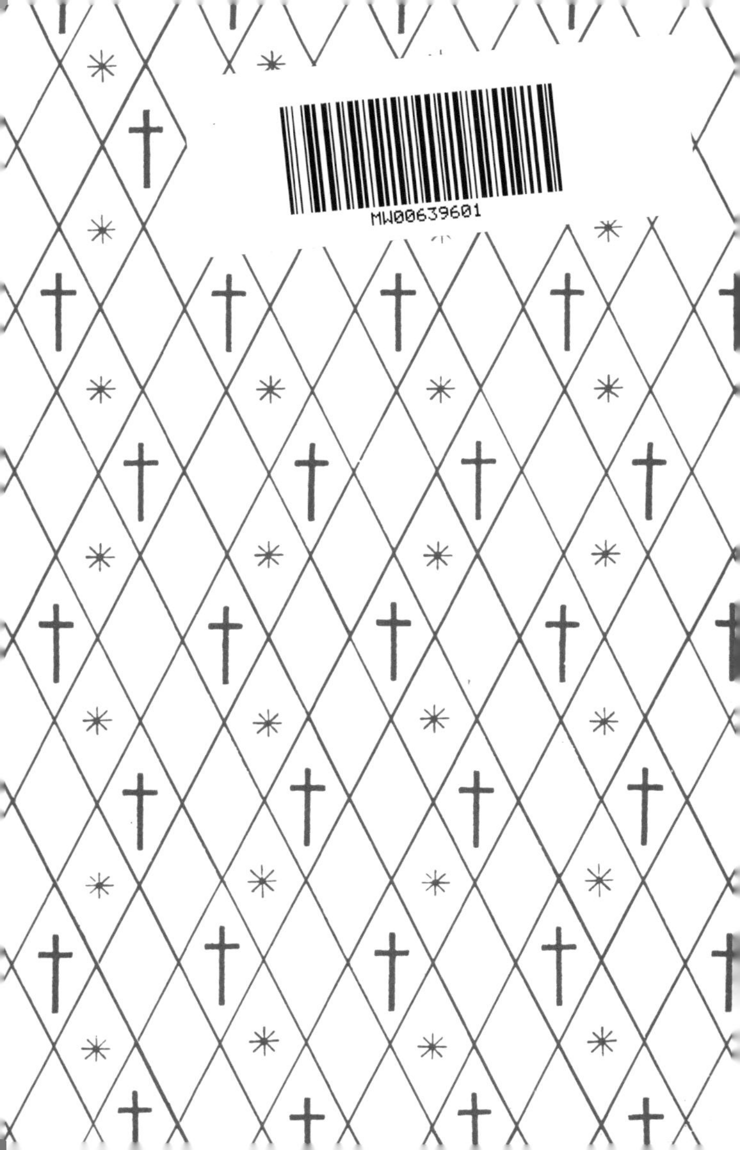
MW00639601

TREASURY OF NOVENAS

Mary and the Apostles in the Upper Room made the first Novena in preparation for the coming of the Holy Spirit.

TREASURY OF NOVENAS

MORE THAN FORTY OF THE MOST POPULAR NOVENAS CAREFULLY ARRANGED FOR PRIVATE PRAYER IN ACCORD WITH THE LITURGICAL YEAR ON THE FEASTS OF JESUS AND MARY AS WELL AS FAVORITE SAINTS

•

With a Short Helpful Meditation Before Each Novena

By

REV. LAWRENCE G. LOVASIK, S.V.D.
Divine Word Missionary

Illustrated in Color

CATHOLIC BOOK PUBLISHING CO.
New Jersey

NIHIL OBSTAT: Francis J. McAree, S.T.D.
Censor Librorum

IMPRIMATUR: ✠ Patrick J. Sheridan, D.D.
Vicar General, Archdiocese of New York

ABBREVIATIONS OF THE BOOKS OF THE BIBLE

Acts—Acts of the Apostles
Am—Amos
Bar—Baruch
1 Chr—1 Chronicles
2 Chr—2 Chronicles
Col—Colossians
1 Cor—1 Corinthians
2 Cor—2 Corinthians
Dan—Daniel
Deut—Deuteronomy
Eccl—Ecclesiastes
Eph—Ephesians
Est—Esther
Ex—Exodus
Ezek—Ezekiel
Ezr—Ezra
Gal—Galatians
Gen—Genesis
Hab—Habakkuk
Hag—Haggai
Heb—Hebrews
Hos—Hosea
Isa—Isaiah
Jas—James
Jdg—Judges
Jer—Jeremiah
Jn—John
1 Jn—1 John
2 Jn—2 John
3 Jn—3 John
Job—Job
Joel—Joel
Jon—Jonah
Jos—Joshua
Jud—Judith
Jude—Jude
1 Ki—1 Kings
2 Ki—2 Kings
Lam—Lamentations
Lev—Leviticus
Lk—Luke
1 Mac—1 Maccabees
2 Mac—2 Maccabees
Mal—Malachi
Mic—Micah
Mk—Mark
Mt—Matthew
Nah—Nahum
Neh—Nehemiah
Num—Numbers
Ob—Obadiah
1 Pet—1 Peter
2 Pet—2 Peter
Phil—Philippians
Philem—Philemon
Prov—Proverbs
Ps(s)—Psalms
Rev—Revelation
Rom—Romans
Ru—Ruth
1 Sam—1 Samuel
2 Sam—2 Samuel
Sir—Sirach
Song—Song of Songs
1 Thes—1 Thessalonians
2 Thes—2 Thessalonians
1 Tim—1 Timothy
2 Tim—2 Timothy
Tit—Titus
Tob—Tobit
Wis—Wisdom
Zec—Zechariah
Zep—Zephaniah

(T-345)

Printed in Korea

FOREWORD

A NOVENA means nine days of public or private prayer for some special occasion or intention. Its origin goes back to the nine days that the disciples and Mary spent together in prayer between Ascension and Pentecost Sunday. Over the centuries many novenas have been highly indulgenced by the Church.

To make a novena means to persevere in prayer asking for some favor over a period of nine days in succession or nine weeks. It means fulfilling our Lord's teaching that we must continue praying and never lose confidence. This confidence is based on our Lord's words:

"Ask and you will receive; seek and you will find; knock and it will be opened to you. For whoever asks receives; whoever seeks finds; whoever knocks is admitted" (Lk 11:9-10).

Many devout Catholics make novenas to God, Our Lady, and the Saints. This book is published to accommodate those who would like to make various novenas and who would like to have them in a single volume. A brief instruction (or meditation) precedes each of these most popular novenas.

The purpose of this collection of novenas is not only to provide prayers to obtain favors from God but also to encourage people to pray frequently because prayer, after the Sacraments, is the richest source of God's grace.

The Liturgy of the Church aids us in our prayer-life. We can keep in touch with the Liturgy by making a novena of prayer at various periods of the Liturgical Year. The Contents are arranged clearly to help in the selection of appropriate prayers for the various Seasons and Feasts of the Church Year.

Try to talk with God during your novena. Absolute sincerity is most important. And as you grow in daily reflection and prayer, you will find yourself talking to God with much the same ease as you would converse with a close friend.

Use your own words in this simple, intimate chat with God, and they will gradually become your own personal, individual way of prayer. You will find that the Holy Spirit is enlightening your mind and strengthening your will to do God's Will.

In order to help you develop this intimate conversation with God, I have added prayers for Spiritual Needs in Part Six.

Father Lawrence G. Lovasik, S.V.D.

CONTENTS

THE NOVENA AND PRAYER

JESUS SPEAKS:

"COME to Me, all you who are weary and overburdened, and I will give you rest. Take My yoke upon you and learn from Me, for I am meek and humble of heart, and you will find rest for your souls. For My yoke is easy and My burden light" (Mt 11:28-30).

"Ask, and it will be given you; seek, and you will find; knock, and the door will be opened to you. For everyone who asks will receive, and those who seek will find, and to those who knock the door will be opened" (Lk 11:9-10).

"Amen, amen, I say to you, if you ask the Father anything in My Name, He will give it to you. Until now, in My Name, you have not asked for anything. Ask and you will receive, so that your joy may be complete" (Jn 16:23-24).

"I am going to the Father. Whatever you ask in My Name I will do, so that the Father may be glorified in the Son. If you ask Me for anything in My Name, I will do it" (Jn 14:12-13).

"When you pray, go into your room, close the door, and pray to your Father in secret. And your Father Who sees everything that is done in secret will reward you" (Mt 6:6).

"Your Father knows what you need before you ask Him" (Mt 6:8).

"Whatever you ask for in prayer and do so with faith, you will receive" (Mt 21:22).

"If you abide in Me, and My words abide in you, you may ask for whatever you wish, and it will be done for you" (Jn 15:7).

"Whoever eats My Flesh and drinks My Blood dwells in Me and I dwell in him" (Jn 6:56).

"Your Father knows what you need before you ask Him. 'This is how you should pray: "Our Father in heaven, hallowed be Your Name. Your Kingdom come. Your will be done on earth as it is in heaven. Give us this day our daily bread. And forgive us our debts as we forgive our debtors. And do not lead us into temptation, but deliver us from the evil one"'" (Mt 6:8-13).

"Stay awake and pray that you may not enter into temptation" (Mt 26:41).

St. Paul Speaks:

"Do not worry about anything, but present your needs to God in prayer and petition, with thanksgiving. Then the peace of God, which is beyond all understanding, will guard your hearts and your minds in Christ Jesus" (Phil 4:6-7).

"In all of your prayers and entreaties, pray in the Spirit on every possible occasion. To that end, keep alert and always persevere in supplication for all the saints" (Eph 6:18).

"Be joyful in your hope. Be patient in times of affliction. Persevere in prayer" (Rom 12:12).

"Rejoice always. Pray continually. Give thanks in all circumstances. For this is the will of God for you in Christ Jesus" (1 Thes 5:16-17).

"Assist us with your prayers, so that thanks may be given to God on our behalf for the blessing granted to us through the prayers of so many" (2 Cor 1:11).

St. James Speaks:

"The devout prayer of an upright person is most effective" (Jas 5:16).

Mary's Prayer:

"My soul proclaims the greatness of the Lord, and my spirit rejoices in God my Savior. For he has looked with favor on the lowliness of His servant; henceforth all generations will call me blessed. The Mighty One has done great things for me, and holy is His Name. His mercy is shown from age to age to those who fear Him" (Lk 1:46-50).

"Blessed be God the Father and His only-begotten Son and the Holy Spirit: for He has shown that He loves us" (Liturgy for Trinity Sunday).

Part One

HOLY TRINITY—FATHER, SON HOLY SPIRIT

God the Father

—ADVENT SEASON—

1. ADVENT NOVENA

MEDITATION

CREATION, including ourselves, is part of a master-plan of the Creator. But when man, created in innocence, finally appeared on the scene, he chose not to cooperate with the mysterious growth into the image of the Creator.

Since all have sinned (Rom 3:23), this "sin of the world" brought about man's inability to realize the divinely-intended freedom into which he is to grow. Hence, Redemption by Jesus, Who took away the sin of the world (Jn 1:29), became necessary. Only in Christ has sinful man the power to become the heavenly man, as intended by God (1 Cor 15:45-49).

Advent is the time of more than usual eager longing, awaiting our revelation as sons of God (Rom 8: 19). It is the waiting for Christ's coming in grace on

Christmas and for His final coming when God's plan will be fully realized in all who have put on Christ by faith and Baptism (Gal 3:27).

God gives us this plan in the words of the Prophets, and the Church gives us their words in Advent. The great precursors were Isaiah and John the Baptist—and others like Baruch, Jeremiah, Zephaniah, and Micah. And then comes Jesus, the fulfillment of all the promises God has made.

From the day of the Annunciation onward, Mary, more than anyone else in the world, had the privilege of knowing that in all truth God is the One Who comes into the world. It is by meditating on the mystery of Christ, "the Son of the Most High," that we begin to understand that He linked our lot with His own by becoming Man and that He will return to inaugurate His eternal Kingdom by saving us.

During Advent, our constant prayer should be: "Come, Lord Jesus!" (Rev 22:20). We should "reject ungodliness and worldly desires, and live temperately, justly, and piously in this age as we await our blessed hope, the appearing of the glory of the great God and of our Savior Jesus Christ" (Tit 2:12-13).

THE WORD OF GOD

"In the beginning was the Word, and the Word was with God, and the Word was God. He was in the beginning with God." —Jn 1:1-2

"No one has ever seen God. It is God the Son, ever at the Father's side, Who has revealed Him." —Jn 1:18

"The Son is the reflection of the Father's glory, the very imprint of His being, and He sustains all things by His all-powerful Word." —Heb 1:3

NOVENA PRAYERS

Novena Prayer

FATHER, all-powerful and ever-living God, I give You thanks through Jesus Christ our Lord. When He humbled Himself to come among us as a Man, He fulfilled the plan You formed long ago and opened for us the way to salvation.

Now I watch for the day, hoping that the salvation promised us will be mine, when Christ our Lord will come again in His glory.

His future coming was proclaimed by all the Prophets. The Virgin Mother bore Him in her womb with love beyond all telling. John the Baptist was His herald and made Him known when at last He came.

In His love He has filled us with joy as we prepare to celebrate His birth. When He comes, may He find me watching in prayer, my heart filled with wonder and praise.

In memory of the coming of our Lord and Savior, I beg You, Father, to grant me all the graces I need to be prepared for His coming to my soul on Christmas. I ask in particular this favor: *(Mention your request).*

For the love Jesus, Your Son, has shown us in becoming Man to save us, I beg You to grant my prayer, if it be Your holy Will.

Prayer to Benefit from Christ's Coming

LORD our God, help me to prepare well for the coming of Christ Your Son. May He find me waiting, eager in joyful prayer.

God of mercy and consolation, help me in my weakness and free me from sin. Hear my prayers that I may rejoice at the coming of Your Son.

You loved the world so much You gave Your only Son to free us from the ancient power of sin and death. Help me who wait for His coming, and lead me to true liberty. Free me from my sins, and make me whole. Hear my prayer, and prepare me to celebrate the Incarnation of Your Son.

Almighty God, help me to look forward to the glory of the birth of Christ our Savior: His coming is proclaimed joyfully in all the world. I await His healing power. Let me not be discouraged by my weaknesses as I prepare for His coming. Keep me steadfast in Your love. Give me the joy of Your love to prepare the way for Him. Help me to serve You and my neighbor.

Father, help me to look forward in hope to the coming of our Savior. May I live as He has taught us, ready to welcome Him with burning love and faith. Let Your glory dawn to take away my darkness, and may I be revealed as a child of light at His coming. Let the light of His coming free me from the darkness of sin and renew His life within me.

My sins bring me unhappiness. Hear my prayer for courage and strength. May the coming of Your Son bring me the joy of salvation. Guide me with Your love as I await His coming. Keep me faithful that I may be helped through life and brought to salvation.

Father, Creator and Redeemer of mankind, You decreed, and Your Word became Man, born of the Virgin Mary. May I come to share the Divinity of Christ, Who humbled Himself to share our human nature. Renew me by the coming feast of Your Son's birth. Give me true faith and love to celebrate the mystery of God made Man. May I who celebrate the birth of Your Son as Man rejoice in the gift of eternal life when He comes in glory. May I share more fully in His Divine life, for He lives and reigns with You and the Holy Spirit, one God, forever. Amen.

Prayer to the Coming Savior

JESUS, our Lord, save me from my sins. Come, protect me from all dangers and lead me to salvation.

Come! Wisdom of our God Most High, guiding creation with power and love: teach me to walk in the paths of knowledge!

Come! Leader of ancient Israel, giver of the Law of Moses on Sinai: rescue me with Your mighty power!

Come! Flower of Jesse's stem, sign of God's love for all His people: save me without delay!

Come! Key of David, opening the gates of God's eternal Kingdom: free the prisoners of darkness!

Come, Emmanuel, God's presence among us, our King, our Judge: save us, Lord our God!

Come, King of all nations, source of Your Church's unity and faith: save all mankind, Your own creation!

Come, Radiant Dawn, splendor of eternal light, Sun of Justice: shine on those lost in the darkness of death!

Come, Lord Jesus, do not delay; give new courage to Your people who trust in Your love. By Your coming, raise us to the joy of Your Kingdom, where You live and reign with the Father and the Holy Spirit, one God, forever. Amen.

2. GOD THE FATHER

MEDITATION

BEFORE the creation and fall of the Angels, before all created things, before all history and before all time, the Divine Word—Himself uncreated and without beginning—lived with His Father in the love of the Holy Spirit.

Saint John tells us what was before His Incarnation. "No one has ever seen God. It is the only Son, God, Who is ever at the Father's side, Who made Him known" (Jn 1:18). He received the sublime doctrine regarding the Divine Word from the teaching of Christ, or by inspiration, or in both ways, for Jesus said, "I have called you friends, because I have revealed to you everything that I have heard from My Father" (Jn 15:15).

We believe that the Son is begotten by the Father; and it is the common teaching that He is begotten through the Divine intellect. "The Word was with God, and the Word was God" (Jn 1:1).

The Father begets the Word because He communicates to this Word a nature not only like, but identical with, His own. Scripture calls the Word, the Son.

The Son ever dwells in the bosom of the Father Who begets Him. He dwells there both by unity of nature and by the love which They mutually bear to one another. From this love proceeds, as from one principle, the Holy Spirit, the substantial love of the Father and the Son. The Divine Nature is one for the Three Persons.

In various proclamations the Father acknowledges Jesus as His Son Who became Man for our salvation. The sky opened and John the Baptist saw the Spirit of God descend like a dove and hover over Jesus. With that, a voice from the heavens said, "This is My beloved Son, in Whom I am well pleased" (Mt 3:17).

At the Transfiguration a voice out of the cloud said, "This is My beloved Son, with Whom I am well pleased. Listen to Him" (Mt 17:5).

The heavenly Father shows us the way to attain to this glorious state that awaits us, the glorious state of Jesus our Head, whose members we are. He said, "Listen to Him!" To listen to Jesus means to accept all that He says to us. Our faith must be put into action by works worthy of a true disciple of Jesus and conformed to the spirit of the Gospel. Then we shall please the Father as His loving children.

In imitation of Jesus, we should give ourselves entirely to our heavenly Father through love and remain united with Him in prayer. God must be not only the principle but also the end of all our works. The heavenly Father took delight in Jesus because all His actions, while in themselves human actions, were Divine in their principle, and were the expression of the most sublime virtues.

Let us ask Jesus, the Divine Word, to show us His Father—His perfections, His greatness, His rights, His Will—so that we may love Him, and He may love us. In this we can imitate God's own Son in honoring our heavenly Father.

THE WORD OF GOD

"The hour is coming, indeed it is already here, when the true worshipers will worship the Father in Spirit and truth. Indeed it is worshipers like these that the Father seeks. God is Spirit, and those who worship Him must worship in Spirit and truth." —Jn 4:23-24

"Your heavenly Father is fully aware of all your needs. . . . Let your main focus be on His Kingdom and His righteousness, and all these things will be given you as well." —Mt 6:32-33

"This is how you should pray: 'Our Father in heaven, hallowed be Your Name. Your Kingdom come. Your will be done on earth as it is in heaven.' " —Mt 6:9-10

NOVENA PRAYERS

Novena Prayer

GOD, my heavenly Father, I adore You, and I count myself as nothing before Your Divine Majesty. You alone are Being, Life, Truth, and Goodness. Helpless and unworthy as I am, I honor You, I praise You, I thank You, and I love You in union with Jesus Christ, Your Son, our Savior and our Brother, in the merciful kindness of His Heart and through His infinite merits.

I desire to serve You, to please You, to obey You, and to love You always in union with Mary Immaculate, Mother of God and our Mother. I also desire to love and serve my neighbor for the love of You.

Heavenly Father, thank You for making me Your child in Baptism. With childlike confidence I ask You for this special favor: *(Mention your request)*.

I ask that Your Will may be done. Give me what You know to be best for my soul, and for the souls of those for whom I pray.

Give me Your Holy Spirit to enlighten me, to correct me, and to guide me in the way of Your commandments and holiness, while I strive for the happiness of heaven where I hope to glorify You forever. Amen.

Offering

ETERNAL Father, I offer You the Sacrifice in which Your dear Son Jesus offered Himself upon the Cross and which He now renews upon the altar: to *adore* You and to render to You that *honor* which is Your due, by acknowledging Your supreme dominion over all things and their complete dependence on You, for You are our first beginning and our last end; to *thank* You for Your countless benefits received; to *appease* Your *justice* provoked to anger by so many sins, and to offer You worthy *atonement* for them; and, finally, to *implore Your grace and mercy* for myself, for all those who are in pain and distress, for all poor sinners, for the whole world, and for the holy souls in purgatory.

For Holy Church

HEAVENLY Father, together with Your Son You sent the Holy Spirit to Your Church and her children, and You continue to send Him to work the wonders of Your Divine love in us.

Enlighten and strengthen through Him our Holy Father and all the bishops and priests of Your Church. Continue to confirm in ever greater holiness all the different states of life and every individual soul within Your Church, and lead her, immaculate Bride of Christ, to victory over all her enemies. Through the same Christ our Lord. Amen.

The Universal Prayer

GOD, my Heavenly Father, I believe in You: increase my faith. I trust in You: strengthen my trust. I love You: let me love You more and more. I am sorry for my sins: deepen my sorrow.

I worship You as my first beginning, I love You as my last end, I praise You as my constant helper, and call on You as my loving protector.

Guide me by Your wisdom, correct me by Your justice, comfort me by Your mercy, protect me by Your power.

I offer You, Lord, my thoughts: to be fixed on You; my words: to have You for their theme; my actions: to reflect my love for You; my sufferings: to be endured for Your greater glory.

I want to do what You ask of me: in the way You ask, for as long as You ask, because You ask it.

Heavenly Father, enlighten my understanding, strengthen my will, purify my heart, and make me holy.

Help me to repent of my past sins, to resist temptation in the future, to rise above my human weaknesses, and to grow stronger as a Christian.

Let me love You, my Lord and my God, and see myself as I really am: a pilgrim in this world, a Christian called to respect and love all whose lives I touch, those in authority over me or those under my authority, my friends and my enemies.

Help me to conquer anger by gentleness, greed by generosity, apathy by fervor. Help me to forget myself and reach out toward others.

Make me prudent in planning, courageous in taking risks, patient in suffering, and unassuming in prosperity.

Keep me, Father, attentive at prayer, temperate in food and drink, diligent in my work, and firm in my good intentions.

Let my conscience be clear, my conduct without fault, my speech blameless, my life well-ordered.

Put me on guard against my human weaknesses; let me cherish Your love for me, keep Your law, and come at last to Your salvation.

Teach me to realize that this world is passing, that my true future is the happiness of heaven, that life on earth is short, and the life to come eternal.

Help me to prepare for death with a proper fear of judgment, but a greater trust in Your goodness. Lead me safely through death to the endless joy of heaven. Grant this through Christ our Lord. Amen.

Prayer

GOD, Heavenly Father, in the Name of Jesus Christ crucified, Your beloved Son, I beg You to forgive all my sins, all my negligences, and all the transgressions of my past life.

God, Heavenly Father, in the Name of Jesus Christ crucified, Your Divine Son, I beg You to grant me the grace to serve You in this life according to Your holy Will.

God, Heavenly Father, in the name of Jesus of Nazareth, Your only-begotten Son, I beg You to have mercy on me at the hour of my death and to receive my soul. Through the same Christ our Lord. Amen.

(St. Francis of Assisi)

God the Son

—CHRISTMAS SEASON—

3. CHRISTMAS NOVENA

MEDITATION

THE mystery of our salvation is to be honored during the Christmas Season, but not as something that happened two thousand years ago—rather as something present. While the act of Christ's birth and manifestation is past, its effects are present. The hidden reality in this mystery is Christ and His saving action. He is present in the mystery of Christmas-Epiphany, constantly interceding for us and communicating Himself in holy symbols.

After the time of waiting in Advent, we enjoy a fuller realization of Christ's presence among us. We should meditate on and celebrate the Christmas mystery as happening now to us and embrace its spiritual effects with an open heart. In the Word made flesh, we see that God is no stranger to the human condition; in the Infant born in a stable to simple working people, we come to understand that God Who is infinitely great is also one of us.

Christmas celebrates the Father's gift to us: the revelation of His loving presence. This knowledge has been given to us through Israel and the prophets and supremely through Christ His Son. It must continue to be made manifest through Christ, living in us.

Christmas is not just a commemoration of our Lord's birth, but the celebration of the great "Emmanuel" (God-is-with-us) mystery. God wants to share our human condition. At Christmas, Christians celebrate the dawn of God's light shining upon man, who goes through a valley of darkness.

The four Christmas Masses, the feast of the Holy Family, the Solemnity of Mary, Mother of God, the Epiphany (Manifestation) of the Lord and His Baptism, show us how God revealed Himself in the Lord Jesus, in Whom He is really "Emmanuel—God with us." In Jesus we see our God made visible and so are caught up in love of the God we cannot see.

THE WORD OF GOD

"While all things were in quiet silence, and the night in the midst of her course, Your all-powerful Word bounded from heaven's royal throne, a fierce warrior into the doomed land." —Wis 18:14-15

"Though He was by nature God, He did not deem equality with God something to be clung to. Rather, He emptied Himself and took the nature of a slave, being born in the likeness of humans." —Phil 2:6-7

"While they were there the days of [Mary's] confinement were completed, and she gave birth to her firstborn Son. She wrapped Him in swaddling clothes and laid Him in a manger."
—Lk 2:6-7

NOVENA PRAYERS

Novena Prayer

HEAVENLY Father, You made Christmas night radiant with the splendor of Jesus Christ our light. I welcome Him as Lord, the true light of the world. Bring me to the joy of His heavenly kingdom.

We are filled with the new light by the coming of Your Word among us. May the light of faith shine in my words and actions.

Lord God, I praise You for creating man, and still more for restoring Him in Christ. Your Son shares our weakness: may I share His glory. Make me faithful to Your Word, that I may bring Your life to others. He made me Your child. May He welcome me into His Kingdom.

God of power and life, glory of all who believe in You, fill the world with Your splendor and show the nations the light of Your truth. May the simple beauty of Jesus' birth summon us always to love what is most deeply human and to see Your Word made flesh reflected in those whose lives we touch.

Father, in the wonder of the Incarnation Your eternal Word has brought to the eyes of faith a new and radiant vision of Your glory. In Him we see You, our God, made visible and so are caught up in love of the God we cannot see.

At Christmas You fill our hearts with joy as we recognize in Christ the revelation of Your love. No eye can see His glory as our God, yet now He is seen as one like us. Christ is Your Son before all ages, yet now He is born in time. He has come to lift up all things to Himself, to restore unity to creation, and to lead mankind from exile into Your heavenly Kingdom.

At Christmas in Jesus a new light has dawned upon the world: God has become one with man, and man has become one again with God. Your eternal Word has taken upon Himself our human weakness, giving our mortal nature immortal value. So marvelous is this oneness between You, our God, and man, that in Christ Man restores to man the gift of everlasting life.

For the love of Jesus, Your Divine Son, Who became Man for us, I beg of You, grant me rich graces during this joyful season of Christmas. I ask especially for this favor: *(Mention your request).*

In honor of the birth of Jesus, grant what I ask if it be Your holy Will.

Prayer to Our Newborn Savior

DIVINE Infant Jesus, with Mary and Joseph I kneel down in devout worship as I gaze upon You lying in Your crib. You wished to enter the world as a Child in order to prove Yourself to be true Man; for by Your weeping and by Your need for rest and nourishment You prove that You have truly taken on human nature. You become human that I may be able to see You, listen to You, imitate You, and unite myself to You.

Even though You are God, You are now able to suffer for us, atone for our sins, and merit graces for our souls. It is through the flesh that man turns away from God; it is in taking on the flesh that You, our God, deliver us.

But You become Man also that man may become like God. In exchange for the humanity which You take from us, You wish to make us share in Your Divinity by sanctifying grace, that You may take complete possession of us.

May the mystery of Your birth bring me the grace to be born anew and live a new, Divine life, more free from sin and from too great an attachment to myself and creatures, a life for God alone.

As it was Mary's joy to form You in her own body, may her joy now be to form You in my soul, so that I may be more like You.

Jesus, I believe that the greatest proof of God's goodness and love toward us is His gift to us of You, His only beloved Son. All love tends to become like that which it loves. You loved man; therefore, You became Man. Infinite love and mercy caused You, the Second Person of the most Holy Trinity, to leave the Kingdom of eternal bliss, to descend from the throne of Your majesty, power, and glory, to become a helpless Child, to suffer and die for us, that we might live.

In Your crib I see the most wondrous love that ever was—the love of God humbling Himself so low to beg the love of our hearts. Give me the grace to love You in return with a deep, true, personal love. I surrender to Your gentle saving influence my heart and mind and will, so that my life may be lived in You, and You may become my intimate daily Companion, Consoler, and Friend.

May I come eagerly and often to unite myself closely to You in Your Sacrament of Love. The church shall be my Bethlehem; the altar, the crib; the sacred species of bread and wine, the swaddling clothes by which I can recognize You as my God, and under which I can, as Mary and Joseph and the shepherds did, take You into my arms; yes, even receive You into my heart—a grace which even the Angels envy me.

Jesus, from the crib You teach the world the true dignity of humility. Poverty, suffering and humiliation stand by Your Cross and by Your crib. Your becoming a child for love of us is the greatest act of humility the world has ever seen. Although heaven and earth cannot contain You, although You are the Creator of all and King of glory, You humble Yourself to such a degree that You need human help. The infinite Lord of all becomes a servant; the Almighty, a helpless creature, the Immortal, mortal. Your Divine love chose this way of raising fallen mankind to its former dignity, for nothing draws the hearts of people so easily to God as Your stooping so low to reach them.

Draw me and all mankind to Yourself by the example of Your loving humility. Teach me that my true glory consists in humbling myself, for You said, "Amen, amen, I say to you, unless you change and become like little children, you will not enter the Kingdom of God" (Mt 18:3).

Prayer to Jesus, God Made Man

JESUS, Son of the glorious Virgin Mary and only Son of the living God, I adore You and acknowledge You as my God, the only true God, one and infinitely perfect. You have made out of nothing all things that are outside of You, and You preserve and govern them with infinite wisdom, sovereign goodness, and supreme power.

I beg of You, by the mysteries that were fulfilled in Your sacred Humanity, to cleanse me in Your Blood from all my past sins. Pour forth abundantly upon me Your Holy Spirit, together with His grace, His virtues, and His gifts. Make me believe in You, hope in You, love You, and labor to merit the possession of You through each of my actions. Give Yourself to me someday in the brightness of Your glory, in the company of Your Blessed Mother, Saint Joseph, and all Your Saints.

4. THE DIVINE INFANT JESUS

MEDITATION

DEVOTION to the Divine Infant encourages people to honor the infancy of Jesus. It is God's will that we honor all the mysteries of our Lord's life so that we may learn to imitate His virtues and make use of the graces which each mystery imparts for our sanctification.

Consequently devotion to the sacred infancy of Jesus is a source of great graces and blessings. It is certainly most pleasing to Jesus that we remember His infinite love in appearing among us in the form of a Child to save our souls and to win our love and confidence. A child attracts love. It is easy to obtain everything from a child.

Devotion to the infancy of Jesus is closely associated with the popular devotion to the Infant Jesus of Prague. It is a devotion to the Son of God, Who came to us in the form of a child. Back in the 17th century the miraculous image of the Infant Jesus was brought to Bohemia by a Spanish princess and presented to a Carmelite monastery. For many years the image was kept on a side altar in the Church of Our Lady of Victory in Prague.

The original wax image stands about nineteen inches high and is clothed in a royal mantle. A jeweled crown rests on its head. Its right hand is raised in blessing, and its left hand holds a globe signifying kingship. The original statue has been called "The Miraculous Infant Jesus of Prague" because so many graces have been received by those who invoked the Infant. Within recent years the devotion to the Miraculous Infant has grown throughout the world.

Our Lord Jesus Christ told us, "Unless you change and become like little children, you will not enter the Kingdom of God" (Mt 18:3). He not only taught us by word but gave His life as an example. He came among us as a helpless Infant to win our love. As a little Child, He was still our God and already by right the King of the Universe He had created and now had come to re-create.

Devotion to our Savior, the Divine Infant, honors the great mystery of His Incarnation. We acknowledge His Divinity and His Humanity, and rejoice in His great love that led Him to give His life for us.

THE WORD OF GOD

"[The shepherds] found Mary and Joseph, and the Baby lying in the manger. When they had seen Him, they understood what had been told them about this Child."

—Lk 2:16-17

"A Child is born to us, and a Son is given to us, and the government is upon His shoulder. And His Name shall be called Wonderful Counselor, Mighty God, Everlasting Father, Prince of Peace." — Isa 9:5

"God so loved the world that He gave His only Son, that whoever believes in Him shall not die but have eternal life. God did not send His Son into the world to condemn the world but to save the world through Him."
—Jn 3:16-17

NOVENA PRAYERS

Novena Prayer

CHILD Jesus, I have recourse to You by Your holy Mother. I implore You to assist me in this need, for I firmly believe Your Divinity can assist me. I confidently hope to obtain Your holy grace. I love You with my whole heart and my whole soul. I am heartily sorry for my sins and beg of You, good Jesus, to give me strength to overcome them.

I make the resolution of never again offending You, and I resolve to suffer everything rather than displease You. Henceforth I wish to serve You faithfully. For the love of You, Divine Child, I will love my neighbor as myself.

Jesus, most powerful Child, I implore You again to help me: *(Mention your request)*.

Divine Child, great omnipotent God, I implore through Your most holy Mother's most powerful intercession, and through the boundless mercy of Your omnipotence as God, for a favorable answer to my prayer during this novena.

Grant me the grace of possessing You eternally with Mary and Joseph and of adoring You with Your holy Angels and Saints. Amen.

Prayer to the Miraculous Infant of Prague

DEAREST Jesus, Little Infant of Prague, how tenderly You love us! Your greatest joy is to dwell among us and to bestow Your blessing upon us. Though I am not worthy that You should help me, I feel drawn to You by love because You are kind and merciful and exercise Your almighty power over me.

So many who turned to You with confidence have received graces and had their petitions granted. Behold me as I come before You to lay open my heart to You with its prayers and hopes. I present to You especially this request, which I enclose in Your loving Heart: *(Mention your request).*

Rule over me, dear Infant Jesus, and do with me and mine according to Your holy Will, for I know that in Your Divine Wisdom and love You will arrange everything for the best. Do not withdraw Your hand from me, but protect and bless me forever.

I pray You, all-powerful and gracious Infant Jesus, for the sake of Your sacred infancy, in the name of Your Blessed Mother Mary who cared for You with such tenderness, and by the greatest reverence with which Saint Joseph carried You in his arms, help me in my needs. Make me truly happy with You, dearest Infant in time and in eternity, and I shall thank You forever with all my heart. Amen.

Prayer

ALMIGHTY and Everlasting God, Lord of heaven and earth, You revealed Yourself to little ones. Grant, we beg of You, that we who venerate with due honor the sacred mysteries of Your Son, the Child Jesus, and imitate His example, may enter the Kingdom of Heaven which You promised to little children. Through the same Christ our Lord. Amen.

Note: The Litany of the Most Holy Name of Jesus may also be said, *p. 47.*

Litany of the Infant Jesus
(For Private Devotion)

LORD, have mercy. *Christ, have mercy.*
Lord, have mercy.
Jesus, hear us.
Jesus, graciously hear us,
God the Father of heaven, *have mercy on us.*
God, the Son, Redeemer of the world,*
God, the Holy Spirit,
Holy Trinity, one God,
Infant, Jesus Christ,
Infant, Son of the living God,
Infant, Son of the Virgin Mary,
Infant, strong in weakness,
Infant, powerful in tenderness,
Infant, treasure of grace,
Infant, fountain of love,
Infant, renewer of the heavens,
Infant, repairer of the evils of earth,
Infant, head of the Angels,
Infant, root of the Patriarchs,

* *Have mercy on us* is repeated after each invocation.

Infant, speech of Prophets,
Infant, desire of the Gentiles,
Infant, joy of shepherds,
Infant, light of the Magi,
Infant, salvation of infants,
Infant, expectation of the just,
Infant, instructor of the wise,
Infant, first-fruits of all Saints,
Be merciful, *spare us, O Infant Jesus.*
Be merciful, *graciously hear us, O Infant Jesus.*
From the slavery of the children of Adam, *Infant Jesus, deliver us.*
From the slavery of the devil,**
From the evil desires of the flesh,
From the malice of the world,
From the pride of life,
From the inordinate desire of knowing,
From the blindness of spirit,
From an evil will,
From our sins,
Through Your most pure Conception,
Through Your most humble Nativity,
Through Your tears,
Through Your most painful Circumcision,
Through Your most glorious Epiphany,
Through Your most pious Presentation,
Through Your most Divine Life,
Through Your poverty,
Through Your many sufferings,
Through Your labors and travels,
Lamb of God, You take away the sins of the world; *have mercy on us, O Infant Jesus.*
Lamb of God, You take away the sins of the world; *graciously hear us, O Infant Jesus.*
Lamb of God, You take away the sins of the world; *have mercy on us.*
℣. Jesus, Infant, hear us.
℟. *Jesus, Infant, graciously hear us.*

****Infant Jesus, deliver us* is repeated after each invocation.

LET us pray. O Lord Jesus Christ, You were pleased so to humble Yourself in Your incarnate Divinity and most sacred Humanity, as to be born in time and become a little child. Grant that we may acknowledge infinite wisdom in the silence of a child, power in weakness, and majesty in humiliation. Adoring Your humiliations on earth, may we contemplate Your glories in heaven, Who with the Father and the Holy Spirit live and reign forever. ℟. *Amen.*

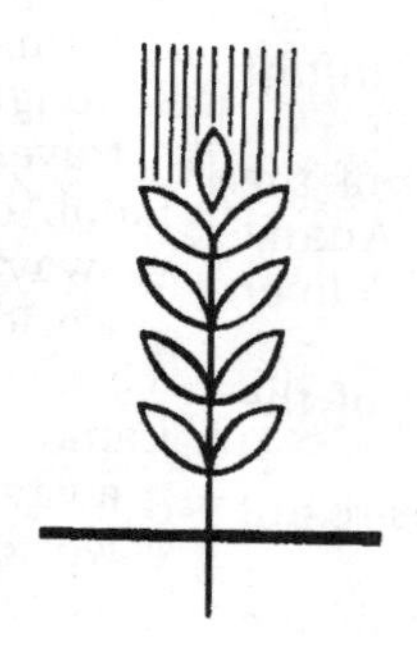

5. THE MOST HOLY NAME OF JESUS

MEDITATION

AMONG the Jews a male child received his name at the rite of circumcision. On the day that the Divine Infant was circumcised, He received the Name of Jesus, which signifies Savior, and which had given Him by the Angel before He was conceived.

The Angel Gabriel said to Mary,"Do not be afraid, Mary, for you have found favor with God. Behold, you will conceive in your womb and bear a Son, and you will name Him Jesus. He will be great and will be called Son of the Most High"(Lk 1:30-31).

The Angel of the Lord appeared in a dream to Joseph and said to him,"Joseph, son of David, do not be afraid to receive Mary into your home as your wife. For this Child has been conceived in her womb through the Holy Spirit. She will give birth to a Son, and you shall name Him Jesus, for He will save His people from their sins"(Mt 1:20-21).

Jesus taught the disciples to present their petitions to the Eternal Father in His Name. "Amen,

amen, I say to you, if you ask the Father for anything in My Name, He will give it to you. Until now, in My Name, you have not asked for anything. Ask, and you will receive, so that your joy may be complete" (Jn 16:23-24). Jesus assured them that by reason of the merits of His redemption, the power of such prayer would be irresistible.

But the greatness of that power would depend largely on their loyalty to and love for Him. Since those who love Jesus remain in Him, prayer offered in His Name is, as it were, His own.

Faith in Jesus and in the power of His Name is the greatest spiritual force in the world today. It is a source of joy and inspiration in our youth; of strength in our manhood, when only His Holy Name and His grace can enable us to overcome temptation; of hope, consolation, and confidence at the hour of our death, when more than ever before, we realize that the meaning of Jesus is "Lord, the Savior." We should bow in reverence to His Name and submission to His holy Will.

In His last discourse with His Apostles He said, "I am going to the Father. Whatever you ask in My Name I will do, so that the Father may be glorified in the Son. Whatever you ask in My Name I will do" (Jn 14:12-13). Our Lord's words are a consolation and encouragement to persevere in prayer. It is good to know on His own testimony that our heavenly Father never grows weary of listening to our petitions. Jesus also assures us that He will grant our prayers if we ask in His Name.

But we must never forget that God may refuse our request, not because He does not love us. He may refuse our request either because what we ask may be harmful to us, or because He has good reason for delaying to grant our petition, or because He desires that we should ask it more urgently. We should submissively adore the wisdom of our God if He altogether withholds the favor we implore.

THE WORD OF GOD

"On the eighth day, when the time for the Child's circumcision had arrived, He was given the Name Jesus, the Name the angel had given Him before He was conceived."
—Lk 2:21

"God greatly exalted [Jesus] and bestowed on Him the Name that is above all other names, so that at the Name of Jesus every knee should bend of those in heaven and on earth, and under the earth, and every tongue should proclaim to the glory of God the Father: Jesus Christ is Lord."
—Phil 2:9-10

"Everyone who calls on the Name of the Lord will be saved."
—Rom 10:13

"Whatever you do in word or deed, do everything in the Name of the Lord Jesus, giving thanks to God the Father through Him."
—Col 3:17

NOVENA PRAYERS

Novena Prayer

JESUS most merciful, in early infancy You began Your office of Savior by shedding Your Precious Blood and assuming for us that Name which is above all names. I thank You for such early proofs of Your infinite love.

I venerate Your sacred Name in union with the deep respect of the Angel who first announced it to the earth. I also unite my affections to the sentiments of tender devotion which Your adorable Name has, in all ages, enkindled in the hearts of Your servants.

Jesus, You said, "If you ask the Father for anything in My Name, He will give it to you" (Jn 16:23). I earnestly ask the Father in Your Name for an increase of faith, hope, and charity, and the grace to lead a good life and to die a happy death.

Jesus, You said, "Whatever you ask in My Name I will do" (Jn 14:13). I earnestly ask You in Your Name to save my soul. I also ask in Your Name for the following favor: *(Mention your request.)*

Jesus, Your most holy Name means "Savior." Be my Savior, dearest Jesus. Mercifully grant me through Your adorable Name—which is the joy of heaven, the terror of hell, the consolation of the afflicted, and the solid ground of my unlimited confidence—all the petitions I make in this prayer.

Blessed Mother of our Redeemer, you shared so closely in the suffering of your dear Son from the moment that He shed His Precious Blood and assumed for us the Name of Jesus, till His last breath on the Cross. Obtain for me and all those I love, as well as for all the faithful, the grace of eternal salvation through the holy Name of Jesus.

Beg also that a most ardent love for Your Divine Son may imprint that sacred Name upon our hearts; that it may be always in our minds, and frequently on our lips; that it may be our defense in temptation, our refuge in danger during our lives, and our consolation and support in the hour of death. Amen.

Contrition

GOOD Jesus, according to Your great mercy, have mercy on me. Most merciful Jesus, by that Precious Blood which You willingly shed for sinners, I beg You to wash away all my sinfulness and to look graciously upon me, a poor and unworthy sinner, as I call upon Your holy Name. Therefore, Jesus, save me for the sake of Your holy Name.

Prayer

GOD, You appointed Your only-begotten Son to be the Savior of mankind, and You commanded His Name to be called Jesus. Mercifully grant that we may enjoy the vision of Him in heaven, whose holy Name we venerate on earth. Through the same Christ our Lord. Amen.

Litany of the Most Holy Name

LORD, have mercy. *Christ, have mercy.*
Lord, have mercy.
Jesus, hear us.
Jesus, graciously hear us.
God, the Father of Heaven, *have mercy on us.**
God the Son, Redeemer of the world,
God, the Holy Spirit,
Holy Trinity, one God,
Jesus, Son of the living God,
Jesus, Splendor of the Father,

**Have mercy on us* is repeated after each invocation, down to *Jesus, Crown of all Saints.*

Jesus, Brightness of eternal Light,
Jesus, King of Glory,
Jesus, Sun of Justice,
Jesus, Son of the Virgin Mary,
Jesus, most amiable,
Jesus, most admirable,
Jesus, the mighty God,
Jesus, Father of the world to come,
Jesus, angel of great counsel,
Jesus, most powerful,
Jesus, most patient,
Jesus, most obedient,
Jesus, meek and humble of heart,
Jesus, Lover of Chastity,
Jesus, our Lover,
Jesus, God of Peace,
Jesus, Author of Life,
Jesus, Model of Virtues,
Jesus, zealous for souls,
Jesus, our God,
Jesus, our Refuge,
Jesus, Father of the Poor,
Jesus, Treasure of the Faithful,
Jesus, good Shepherd,
Jesus, true Light,
Jesus, eternal Wisdom,
Jesus, infinite Goodness,
Jesus, our Way and our Life,
Jesus, joy of the Angels,
Jesus, King of the Patriarchs,
Jesus, Master of the Apostles,
Jesus, Teacher of the Evangelists,
Jesus, Strength of Martyrs,
Jesus, Light of Confessors,
Jesus, Purity of Virgins,
Jesus, Crown of all Saints,

Be merciful, *spare us, O Jesus!*

Be merciful, graciously hear us, O Jesus.

From all evil, *deliver us, O Jesus.***
From all sin,
From Your wrath,
From the snares of the devil,
From the spirit of fornication,
From everlasting death,
From the neglect of Your inspirations,
Through the mystery of Your holy Incarnation,
Through Your Nativity,

***Deliver us, O Jesus*, is repeated after each invocation down to *Through Your Glory*.

Through Your Infancy,
Through Your most Divine Life,
Through Your Labors,
Through Your Agony and Passion,
Through Your Cross and Dereliction,
Through Your Sufferings,
Through Your Death and Burial,
Through Your Resurrection,
Through Your Ascension,
Through Your Institution of the Most Holy Eucharist,
Through Your Joys,
Through Your Glory,
Lamb of God, You take away the sins of the world; *spare us, O Jesus!*
Lamb of God, You take away the sins of the world; *graciously hear us, O Jesus!*
Lamb of God, You take away the sins of the world; *have mercy on us, O Jesus!*
℣. Jesus, hear us.
℟. *Jesus, graciously hear us.*

LET us pray. O Lord Jesus Christ, You have said, "Ask, and you shall receive; seek, and you shall find; knock, and it shall be opened to you"; mercifully attend to our supplications, and grant us the grace of Your most Divine love, that we may love You with all our hearts, and in all our words and actions, and never cease to praise You.

Make us, O Lord, to have a perpetual fear and love of Your holy Name, for You never fail to govern those whom You solidly establish in Your love. You, Who live and reign forever and ever. ℟. *Amen.*

6. THE HOLY FAMILY

MEDITATION

ALL that the Gospels tell us of Christ's hidden life at Nazareth with Mary and Joseph is that He "was obedient to them," and that "Jesus increased in wisdom and in age and in grace with God and men" (Lk 2:52). Jesus could say of His Mother and foster father what He said of His heavenly Father: "I do always the things that please them." Out of a life of thirty-three years, Jesus, Who is Eternal Wisdom, chose to pass thirty years in silence and obscurity, obedience and labor. Truly, He is a hidden God. It was in this hidden life of Nazareth that Mary had the rare privilege of observing the example of her Divine Son and of becoming more like Him in grace and virtue.

The Holy Family is a model for all Christian families. In the family life of Jesus, Mary, and Joseph are exemplified the proper relations that should exist between husband and wife, parents and children. There was filial devotion to God in that family circle of the three holiest persons who ever lived. While Joseph supported the Holy Family by handwork, Mary managed the household, and Jesus assisted both of them. They were united in their daily tasks, which they made holy by prayer and meditation. By practicing the domestic virtues of charity, obedience, and mutual help, they sanctified family life. We should often pray to them to sanctify our families by their example and intercession.

In their Pastoral Letter on the Blessed Virgin (November 21, 1973) the Catholic Bishops of the United States stated: "What does Mary mean to today's family? Mother of the Holy Family at Nazareth, Mary is mother and queen of every Christian family.

"When Mary conceived and gave birth to Jesus, human motherhood reached its greatest achievement. From the time of the Annunciation, she was the living chalice of the Son of God made Man. In the tradition of her people she recognized that God gives life and watches over its growth.

"God called Mary and Joseph to sublimate the consummation of their married love in exclusive dedication to the Holy Child, conceived not by a human father but by the Holy Spirit. When Mary said to Gabriel, 'How can this be since I do not know man?' (Lk 1:34), the Angel told her of the virginal conception. Joseph received the same message in a dream. Christian tradition from early times has seen Saint Joseph as protector of the Christ Child and of his wife's consecrated virginity throughout their married life.

"Mary is Queen of the home. As a woman of faith, she inspires all mothers to transmit the Christian faith to their children. In the setting of family love, children should learn free and loving obedience, inspired by Mary's obedience to God."

THE WORD OF GOD

"When Joseph and Mary had fulfilled everything required by the Law of the Lord, they returned to Galilee, to their own town of Nazareth. The Child grew and became strong, filled with wisdom, and God's favor was upon Him." —Lk 2:39-40

"After the death of Herod, an Angel of the Lord suddenly appeared in a dream to Joseph in Egypt and said, 'Arise, take the Child and His Mother, and go to the land of Israel, for those who had sought to kill the Child are dead.' Joseph got up, took the Child and His Mother, and returned to the land of Israel." —Mt 2:19-21

"After three days they found [the Boy Jesus] in the temple, where he was sitting among the teachers, listening to them and asking them questions. And all who heard Him were amazed at His intelligence and His answers. . . . Then He went down with them and came to Nazareth, and He was obedient to them. . . . And Jesus increased in wisdom and in age and in grace with God and men." —Lk 2:46-47, 51-52

NOVENA PRAYERS

Novena Prayer

JESUS, Mary, and Joseph, bless me and grant me the grace of loving Holy Church as I should, above every earthly thing, and of ever showing my love by deeds.

Jesus, Mary, and Joseph, bless me and grant me the grace of openly professing as I should, with courage and without human respect, the faith that I received as your gift in holy Baptism.

Jesus, Mary, and Joseph, bless me and grant me the grace of sharing as I should in the defense and propagation of the Faith when duty calls, whether by word or by the sacrifice of my possessions and my life.

Jesus, Mary, and Joseph, bless me and grant me the grace of loving my family and others in mutual charity as I should, and establish us in perfect harmony of thought, will, and action, under the rule and guidance of the shepherds of the Church.

Jesus, Mary, and Joseph, bless me and grant me the grace of conforming my life fully as I should to the commandments of God's law and those of His Holy Church, so as to live always in that charity which they set forth.

Jesus, Mary, and Joseph, I ask in particular this special favor: *(Mention your favor).*

Dedication of One's Family

MOST loving Jesus, by Your sublime and beautiful virtues of humility, obedience, poverty, modesty, charity, patience, and gentleness You blessed with peace and happiness the family which You chose on earth. In Your mercy look upon my family. We belong to You, for we have received Your many blessings over many years and we entrust ourselves to Your loving care.

Look upon my family in Your loving kindness, preserve us from danger, give us help in time of need, and grant us the grace to persevere to the end in imitation of Your holy Family, so that having revered You and loved You faithfully on earth, we may praise You eternally in heaven.

Mary, dearest Mother, to your intercession we have recourse, knowing that your Divine Son will hear your prayers. Glorious patriarch, Saint Joseph, help us by your powerful prayers and offer our prayers to Jesus through Mary's hands. Amen.

Prayer

LORD Jesus Christ, being subject to Mary and Joseph, You sanctified family life by Your beautiful virtues. Grant that we, with the help of Mary and Joseph, may be taught by the example of Your holy Family, and may after death enjoy its everlasting companionship.

Lord Jesus, help us ever to follow the example of Your holy Family, that in the hour of our death Your glorious Virgin Mother together with Saint Joseph may come to meet us, and we may be worthy to be received by You into the everlasting joys of heaven. You live and reign forever. Amen.

—SEASON OF LENT—

7. LENTEN NOVENA

MEDITATION

ACCORDING to Biblical tradition, Moses stayed on Mount Sinai forty days to receive the Law of the Covenant. Our Lord fasted forty days in the desert before He started His mission. Christians prepare themselves to celebrate the Paschal Mystery of our Lord's Death and Resurrection by a penitential season of forty days.

Penance is part of the Christian philosophy of life. It has to do with sin and conversion. It is the inner aversion to evil in and around us and a generous conversion in love to God which is important.

The means to achieve this inner conversion are the traditional Lenten practices of prayer, charitable works, and acts of self-denial, but above all attendance at Holy Mass daily because it is a memorial as well as a reenactment of the sacrifice of Christ on

Calvary. What we "give up" should be related to an inner conversion to God.

Jesus came into the world to share His life with us. We should examine the priorities in our lives with His mission in mind. His mission is to bring each person to human dignity, and all people to brotherhood, leading them to the Father. He sought to do the will of His Father.

Lent is a time of instruction and listening. Faith comes by hearing, which certainly includes reading and study. It is a time of listening. The Word of God is given to us in abundance. The Gospels and Lenten Readings are a rich source of faith, conversion, and turning back to a God Who is already awaiting and loving us. We are asked to make the Word of God a judgment upon our lives and a means of personal evaluation.

But this will become fruitful only by the grace of God which we receive through Sacraments and prayer, especially through the Sacrifice of the Mass. Meditation on the Passion of Christ is a favorite means of showing our gratitude to our Lord for having suffered and died for us. The Way of the Cross should not be considered outdated. Making a Lenten Novena at least once during Lent will prove very beneficial in deepening our prayer-life.

THE WORD OF GOD

"We beg you not to receive the grace of God in vain. For He says, 'In an acceptable time I have heard you; on a day of salvation I have helped you.' Behold, now is the acceptable time! Behold, now is the day of salvation!"

— 2 Cor 6:1-2

"This, rather, is the fast I wish: release those bound unjustly, loose the thongs of the yoke; set free the

oppressed, break every yoke. Share your food with the hungry, shelter the oppressed and the homeless; clothe the naked when you see them, and do not turn your back on your own."
—Isa 58:6-7

"Behold, I stand, knocking at the door. If you hear Me calling and open the door, I will enter your house and have supper with you, and you with Me. I will give the victor the right to sit with Me on My throne."
—Rev 3:20-21

NOVENA PRAYERS

Novena Prayer

FATHER, all-powerful and ever-living God, during the Holy Season of Lent You call us to a closer union with Yourself. Help me to prepare to celebrate the Paschal Mystery with mind and heart renewed. Give me a spirit of loving reverence for You, our Father, and of willing service to my neighbor. As I recall the great events that gave us new life in Christ, bring the image of Your Son to perfection within my soul.

This great season of grace is Your gift to Your family to renew us in spirit. Give me strength to purify my heart, to control my desires, and so to serve You in freedom. Teach me how to live in this passing world with my heart set on the world that will never end.

I ask for the grace to master my sinfulness and conquer my pride. I want to show to those in need Your goodness to me by being kind to all.

Through my observance of Lent, help me to correct my faults and raise my mind to You, and thus grow in holiness that I may deserve the reward of everlasting life.

In Your mercy grant me this special favor: *(Mention your request).*

The days of the life-giving Death and glorious Resurrection of Jesus Christ, Your Son, are approaching. This is the hour when He triumphed over Satan's pride, the time when we celebrate the great event of our Redemption. The Suffering and Death of Your Son brought life to the whole world, moving our hearts to praise Your glory.

The power of the Cross reveals Your judgment on this world and the kingship of Christ crucified. Father, through His love for us and through His Sufferings, Death and Resurrection, may I gain eternal life with You in heaven.

Prayer for Spiritual Renewal

GOD, heavenly Father, look upon me and hear my prayer during this holy Season of Lent. By the good works You inspire, help me to discipline my body and to be renewed in spirit.

Without You I can do nothing. By Your Spirit help me to know what is right and to be eager in doing Your will. Teach me to find new life through penance. Keep me from sin, and help me live by Your commandment of love.

God of love, bring me back to You. Send Your Spirit to make me strong in faith and active in good works. May my acts of penance bring me Your forgiveness, open my heart to Your love, and prepare me for the coming feast of the Resurrection of Jesus.

Lord, during this Lenten Season nourish me with Your Word of life and make me one with You in love and prayer.

Fill my heart with Your love and keep me faithful to the Gospel of Christ. Give me the grace to rise above my human weakness. Give me new life by Your Sacraments, especially the Mass.

Father, our source of life, I reach out with joy to grasp Your hand; let me walk more readily in Your ways. Guide me in Your gentle mercy, for left to myself I cannot do Your Will.

Father of love, source of all blessings, help me to pass from my old life of sin to the new life of grace. Prepare me for the glory of Your Kingdom.

I ask this through our Lord Jesus Christ, Your Son, Who lives and reigns with You and the Holy Spirit, one God, forever. Amen.

Prayer

ALMIGHTY and Everlasting God, You have given the human race Jesus Christ our Savior as a model of humility. He fulfilled Your

Will by becoming Man and giving His life on the Cross. Help us to bear witness to You by following His example of suffering and make us worthy to share in His Resurrection. We ask this through our Lord Jesus Christ, Your Son. Amen.

The Way of the Cross

First Station

Jesus Condemned to Death

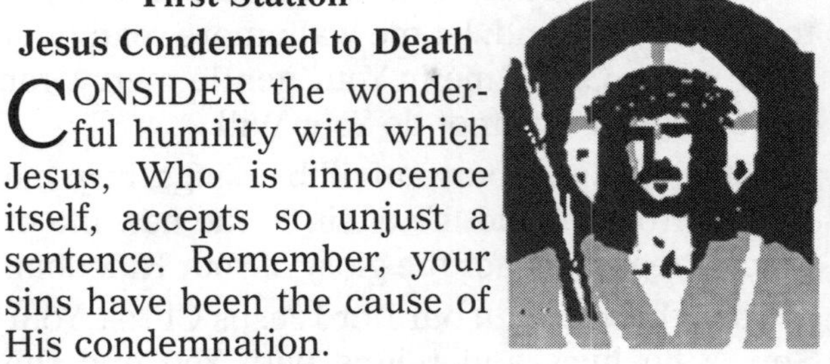

CONSIDER the wonderful humility with which Jesus, Who is innocence itself, accepts so unjust a sentence. Remember, your sins have been the cause of His condemnation.

Most loving Jesus, for the sake of so unworthy a creature as I am, You have suffered so much, and to crown all You have been condemned to a most shameful death. Surely this is enough to touch my heart and make me detest my sins. I bitterly repent of them and will continue to be sorry for having committed them.

Second Station
Jesus Carries the Cross

SEE with what love Jesus embraces the Cross. How patiently He bears the mistreatment of the executioners and the wrath of the people! And you impatiently shrink from the slightest suffering. Without the Cross no one can enter heaven.

Jesus, this Cross should be mine and not Yours, for it was prepared by my sins. Dearest Savior, give me strength to embrace all the crosses which my many sins deserve. Grant that I may die embracing the holy Cross.

Third Station
Jesus Falls the First Time

JESUS, weakened by the continual shedding of His Blood, falls to the ground for the first time. See how His brutal executioners assail Him with blows, kicks, and stripes. Yet our most patient Lord does not open His lips, but suffers in silence. And you complain at the least trouble.

Fourth Station
Jesus Meets His Mother

WHAT sorrow pierces the Heart of Jesus and what pain wounds the heart of Mary in this meeting! Mary, full of affliction, seems to say, "Give up the sins which have caused our pain and sorrow."

Mother of sorrows, behold me at your feet, humbled and filled with contrition. I am the traitor whose sins made the sword of sorrow which pierced your most tender heart. I sincerely repent of all my sins and ask for pardon and mercy. Help me that I may sin no more.

Fifth Station
Simon Helps Jesus

CONSIDER that you are Simon who is helping to carry the Cross against his will. Relieve your God of so great a burden by accepting with good will the troubles which come to you from the hand of God.

My dearest Jesus, You give me so many opportunities of suffering for You and of meriting an eternal reward.

Give me the grace to bear patiently that which seems evil in this life that I may lay up a treasure of eternal good in the next.

Sixth Station
Veronica Wipes the Face of Jesus

CONSIDER the sorrowful image of Jesus imprinted on that cloth, and lovingly strive to form a lively picture of it in your heart. Happy will you be if you live with Jesus imprinted upon your heart, and blessed if you die with Jesus engraver there.

My Savior, I beg of You to impress deeply upon my heart the image of Your sacred Face that I may always think of You and with Your most sorrowful Passion before my eyes ever repent of my sins, the cause of Your sufferings.

Seventh Station
Jesus Falls the Second Time

CONSIDER Jesus lying on the hard ground, weighed down by His sorrows, trampled under foot by His enemies, and derided by the crowd. Remember that it is your pride and self-love that made Him fall. Be sincerely sorry for your past sins and resolve for the future to humble yourself.

Most holy Redeemer, although I see You fallen, I acknowledge You to be Almighty God. I beg of You, banish all my proud thoughts and my self-love that I may ever humbly and willingly embrace suffering and contempt.

Eighth Station
Jesus Speaks to the Women of Jerusalem

YOU have a double cause to weep—both for Jesus Who suffers so much for you and for yourself who ungratefully offend Him so often.

STATIONS *of the* CROSS

1. Jesus is Condemned to Death

O Jesus, help me to appreciate Your sanctifying grace more and more.

2. Jesus Bears His Cross

O Jesus, You chose to die for me. Help me to love You always with all my heart.

3. Jesus Falls the First Time

O Jesus, make me strong to conquer my wicked passions, and to rise quickly from sin.

4. Jesus Meets His Mother

O Jesus, grant me a tender love for Your Mother, who offered You for love of me.

STATIONS *of the* CROSS

5. Jesus is Helped by Simon

O Jesus, like Simon lead me ever closer to You through my daily crosses and trials.

6. Jesus and Veronica

O Jesus, imprint Your image on my heart that I may be faithful to You all my life.

7. Jesus Falls a Second Time

O Jesus, I repent for having offended You. Grant me forgiveness of all my sins.

8. Jesus Speaks to the Women

O Jesus, grant me tears of compassion for Your sufferings and of sorrow for my sins.

STATIONS *of the* CROSS

9. Jesus Falls a Third Time

O Jesus, let me never yield to despair. Let me come to You in hardship and spiritual distress.

10. He is Stripped of His Garments

O Jesus, let me sacrifice all my attachments rather than imperil the divine life of my soul.

11. Jesus is Nailed to the Cross

O Jesus, strengthen my faith and increase my love for You. Help me to accept my crosses.

12. Jesus Dies on the Cross

O Jesus, I thank You for making me a child of God. Help me to forgive others.

13. Jesus is Taken down from the Cross

O Jesus, through the intercession of Your holy Mother, let me be pleasing to You.

14. Jesus is Laid in the Tomb

O Jesus, strengthen my will to live for You on earth and bring me to eternal bliss in heaven.

Prayer after the Stations

JESUS, You became an example of humility, obedience and patience, and preceded me on the way of life bearing Your Cross. Grant that, inflamed with Your love, I may cheerfully take upon myself the sweet yoke of Your Gospel together with the mortification of the Cross and follow You as a true disciple so that I may be united with You in heaven. Amen.

Dearest Savior, fill my heart with deep repentance. Help me to meditate on Your sufferings frequently that I may learn to love You more. Look upon me with eyes of mercy in this life so that I may behold You in peace at the moment of my death.

Ninth Station
Jesus Falls the Third Time

BEHOLD with what cruelty the Lamb of God is beaten by His executioners. See how they bruise and drag Him in the dust. How horrible is sin, which has thus mistreated the Son of God!

My God, You are almighty. Heaven and earth are sustained by You. My frequent sins have made You fall so painfully to the ground. Behold me now, contrite at Your feet, fully resolved never to offend You again.

Tenth Station
Jesus Is Stripped of His Garments

JESUS, covered with bruises and wounds, is tormented with the bitter drink of gall. He atones for intemperance and sensuality.

Jesus, You are covered with blood, wounds, and bitterness while I enjoy comfort, pleasure, and sweetness.

I beg of You, dearest Lord, make me change my life, and let me always remember Your sufferings offered to save my soul.

Eleventh Station
Jesus Is Nailed to the Cross

CONSIDER the terrible pain which Jesus, our Savior, suffers when the nails pierce and tear His veins, bones, nerves, and flesh. Your sins have caused this pain.

Jesus, crucified for my sake, wound my heart with Your holy fear and love. Grant that I may now crucify all my evil desires so that I may have the happiness of living and dying crucified with You and thus come to reign gloriously with You in heaven.

Twelfth Station
Jesus Dies on the Cross

LOOK at your loving Savior hanging on the Cross, fastened by nails. Hear how He prays for His enemies, promises paradise to the good thief, leaves His Mother to the care of John, recommends His Soul to His heavenly Father, and finally, bowing His head, dies. Jesus is dead on the Cross for you!

My dearest Redeemer, I do not deserve to be pardoned, for I am the unfortunate one who has joined Your executioners. But what consolation for me to hear You praying for those who crucified You! What shall I do for You, Who have done so much for me? I am willing to accept whatever You may wish. Grant that I may hear You say to me in my last moments: "Today you will be with Me in Paradise."

Thirteenth Station
Jesus Is Taken Down from the Cross

CONSIDER what a sword of sorrow pierced the heart of our afflicted Mother when she received the lifeless body of her Son into her arms. But the sharpest sword which pierced her heart was sin—sin, which deprived her dearest Son of life. Be truly sorry for your own sins.

Queen of Martyrs, when shall I be worthy to understand your sorrows and keep them ever before my mind? Mother of sorrows, grant that I may have deep contrition for my sins, which have caused you so much suffering, so that, in love and repentance, I may die with God's forgiveness and live forever with you.

Fourteenth Station
Jesus Is Laid in the Tomb

CONSIDER the sadness of Mary's afflicted heart when she was entirely separated from her most loving Son. At the sight of her tears you will realize how little compassion you have for the bitter sufferings of your Savior.

Merciful Jesus, for love of me You have willed to make this sorrowful journey. I adore You reposing in the tomb. United to You, may I rise to a new life. By Your sacred Passion, grant that I may receive Your holy Body as Viaticum and let my last words be: "Jesus and Mary."

Prayer

GOD, for our sake You willed that Your Son should undergo the torments of the Cross so that You might drive far from us the power of the enemy. Grant us, Your servants, that we may attain to the grace of His Resurrection.

Lord Jesus Christ, Son of the living God, at the sixth hour You mounted the gibbet of the Cross for the redemption of the world and shed Your Precious Blood for the remission of our sins. We humbly beg of You that You grant us the grace after death to enter with joy the gates of heaven, for You live and reign forever. Amen.

8. JESUS CRUCIFIED

MEDITATION

THE greatest of God's works is the taking on of human flesh by His Son, Jesus Christ, and this is called the Incarnation.

The Son came on earth to bring the world His own Divine Life and to save it from sin and in this way to make the world new again from within. Jesus offered His life as the highest gift to His Father by dying on the Cross for us. In this way He redeemed the world. The Passion and Death of our Lord teaches us the great evil of sin. It was sin which caused Him to suffer so much and to die. But he took away our sins and made us free to serve God and to reach heaven.

Jesus Christ is our Savior because through Him all creatures will be saved from the slavery of sin. There is no salvation in anyone but Jesus Christ, nor has there ever been.

Jesus Christ is our Savior and Redeemer because as God made Man He preached the Gospel of the Kingdom of God and gave Himself up to death out of love for His Father and for us.

God sent His Son to free men from the power of Satan and made peace between God and men. To do this Jesus had to become man, to preach His truth about the Kingdom of His Father. He continued preaching even though some of the religious leaders of His nation were trying to harm Him. They finally arranged to have Him put to death by the Romans because He claimed to be the Son of God. He is truly our Savior.

Jesus is also our Redeemer because He paid our debt for sin and bought heaven back for us. He offered His life for the love of us and for the glory of His Father. He did His Father's Will to honor Him and to make people happy forever in God's Kingdom. The Father now gives His own Divine Life of grace to people who turn to Him in Faith.

We show our love for Jesus when we remember how much He suffered for us. We can do this during the Holy Season of Lent, each Friday of the week, but above all at Holy Mass, because the Eucharistic celebration is carried out in obedience to His words at the Last Supper: "Do this in memory of Me."

THE WORD OF GOD

"No one can have greater love than to lay down his life for his friends." —Jn 15:13

"[God] did not spare His own Son but gave Him up for all of us. How then can He fail also to give us everything else along with Him?" —Rom 8:32

(The Seven Last Words)

1. "Father, forgive them, for they do not know what they are doing" (Lk 23:34).
2. "Amen, I say to you, today you will be with Me in paradise" (Lk 23:43)
3. "Woman, behold your Son" (Jn 19:26).
4. "My God, My God, why have You forsaken Me?" (Mt 27:46).
5. "I thirst" (Jn 19:28).
6. "It is finished" (Jn 19:30).
7. "Father, into Your hands I commend My spirit" (Lk 23:46).

NOVENA PRAYERS

Novena Prayer

JESUS Christ, Son of God made Man, crowned with thorns, bearing a scepter of a reed, wearing a royal cloak purpled with Your Precious Blood, I venerate You as the Man of Sorrows and acknowledge You as my Lord and King!

Jesus crucified, I firmly renounce the devil and detest all sin that has torn me from Your loving friendship. I pledge my loyalty to You, my Savior, and beg You to make me Your own in sincerest love. I promise to be faithful in serving You, and to strive to become more pleasing to You by avoiding every sin and its occasions, by carrying out my duties perfectly as a good Catholic, and by practicing virtue.

Jesus crucified, accept the homage I wish to render You during this novena, as a token of my sincerest appreciation for the sorrows and sufferings You have willingly borne to atone for my many sins and to prove how much You love me.

I adore You as my very God, Who willed to become Man in order to save me from eternal death.

I thank You as my best Friend, Who laid down Your life as proof of the greatest love possible.

I ask pardon for having so little thought of You, Jesus crucified, and for having caused Your sorrows and sufferings by the many sins I have committed.

I pray to You, dearest Jesus, for all the graces I need to know You, to love You and serve You faithfully until death, and to save my soul. Give me a tender and fervent devotion to Your Sacred Passion by which I was redeemed, venerating You especially in Holy Mass. Teach me how to unite the sorrows and sufferings of my life with Your own.

Finally, through all Your sorrows and pains, through your Sacred Heart glowing with love for me, broken because of my want of love for You, through the sorrows of Mary, your Sorrowful Mother, I ask for this special favor: *(Mention your request).*

With childlike trust I abandon myself to Your holy Will concerning my request.

9. THE MOST PRECIOUS BLOOD OF JESUS

MEDITATION

CATHOLIC theology teaches that the entire human nature of Christ is worthy of adoration because of its intimate and unending union with the Person of the Divine Word. Devotion to any one of the parts of the human nature of Christ properly takes the form of adoration. The motive of such adoration is the Godhead itself, or the Divine Word, Who is inseparably united with Christ's sacred Humanity.

But there are certain parts of Christ's human nature which are particularly deserving of honor because of the singular part they played in the mystery of Redemption or because of a special symbolism they possess. The special reason underlying devotion to the Most Precious Blood of Christ is the fact that we were redeemed with the Precious Blood. The Precious Blood of Christ, shed to the last drop during the Passion, is the price He paid for our salvation.

The Blood of Christ is true sacrificial blood shed to ratify the New Covenant. His Blood was far more excellent than the blood of sacrificial victims of the Old Covenant to cleanse and purify us. By the Will of God and according to His Divine plan, the New Covenant required dedication by the blood of a victim, Jesus Christ. At the Last Supper Jesus said, "This cup is the New Covenant in My Blood, which will be poured out for you" (Lk 22:20). As a reward for the Blood, which Jesus shed in establishing an everlasting Covenant, the Eternal Father raised Him from the dead, and thus His bloody Death on the Cross merited for Him, as well as for us, a glorious Resurrection.

The Precious Body and Blood of Christ is offered in the Mass as the sacrifice of Christ's Mystical Body, as the sacrifice of each of us.

The Precious Body and Blood of Christ received in Holy Communion gives food, drink, refreshment, and health to the life of the soul. The Lamb of God, slain for the sins of mankind, is the sacrifice and the banquet of the Christian soul, the very strength and inspiration for Christian living. Thus devotion to the Most Precious Blood encourages a greater love for the Mass.

The Blood of Christ is real drink and, together with His flesh, is food for our eternal life. Jesus promised the Eucharist in these words: "Whoever eats My Flesh and drinks My Blood has eternal life, and I will raise him up on the last day. For My Flesh is real food and My Blood is real drink. Whoever eats My Flesh and drinks My Blood dwells in Me, and I dwell in him" (Jn 6:54-56).

St. Paul says, "Whenever you eat this Bread and drink this Cup, you proclaim the Death of the

Lord until He come!" (1 Cor 11:26). "The Cup of blessing that we bless, is it not a sharing in the Blood of Christ?" (1 Cor 10:16).

The Precious Blood of Jesus was symbolized by the victims of the Old Law; yet this Blood alone, by virtue of its infinite efficacy, can wash us free from all sin and sanctify us if we avail ourselves of the Sacraments which our Savior has given us, especially the Sacrament of Penance and the Holy Eucharist.

A single drop of the Blood of Jesus would have sufficed to save us, for being the God-Man, everything in Him is of Infinite value. But it was to manifest to us the extent of His love that He shed His Blood to the last drop when His Sacred Heart was pierced. Now, if He shed His very life's blood for us, it is but right that we live only for Him.

THE WORD OF GOD

"One of the soldiers thrust a lance into His side, and immediately a flow of Blood and water came out."

—Jn 19:34

"Now Christ has arrived as the High Priest of all the good things that have come to be. He has passed through the greater and more perfect tabernacle not made by human hands, that is, not a part of this creation, and he has entered once for all into the sanctuary not with the blood of goats and calves but with His own Blood, thus obtaining eternal redemption." —Heb 9:11-12

"You are well aware that you were ransomed from your futile way of life inherited from your ancestors not with perishable things like silver or gold, but with the precious Blood of Christ." —1 Pet 1:18-19

"You are worthy to receive the scroll and to break its seals, for You were slain, and with Your Blood You purchased for God people of every tribe and language, nation and race. You made them into a kingdom and priests to serve our God, and they will reign on earth."

—Rev 5:9-10

NOVENA PRAYERS

Novena Prayer

JESUS, Man of Sorrows, accept the homage I wish to render Your most Precious Blood during this novena, as a token of my sincerest appreciation for the sorrows and sufferings You have willingly borne to atone for my many sins and to prove how much You love me.

I adore You as my very God, Who willed to become Man in order to save me from eternal death.

I thank you as the best Friend I have, Who laid down Your life as proof of the greatest love possible.

I ask pardon for having so little thought of You, the Man of Sorrows, and for having caused Your sorrows and sufferings by the many sins I have committed.

I pray to You, good Jesus, for all the graces I need to know You, to love You and serve You faithfully until death, and to save my soul. Give me a fervent devotion to Your Sacred Passion by which I was redeemed, venerating especially Your Precious Blood. Teach me how to unite the sorrows and sufferings of my life with Your own.

Through the merits of Your most Precious Blood and the prayers of Your Mother of Sorrows, I ask for this special favor: *(Mention your request).*

With childlike trust I abandon myself to Your holy Will concerning my request. If it should not please You to grant what I ask, I beg You, give me that which You know will be of greater benefit to my soul.

Grant me the grace to know You, to love You, and to be truly sorry that I have offended You. I ask this grace by Your Precious Blood:

By that Precious Blood which bathed Your sacred Body and trickled down to the ground in the Garden of Olives.

By that Precious Blood which poured forth from Your sacred Body during the scourging.

By that Precious Blood which covered Your Sacred Face when You were crowned with thorns.

By that Precious Blood which burst from Your hands and feet on Calvary.

By that Precious Blood which came forth from Your Sacred Heart after Your Death.

By that Precious Blood which is still offered daily on our altars at Holy Mass.

By that Precious Blood which we drink in Holy Communion and of which You said, "He who feeds on My Flesh and drinks My Blood has life eternal."

Offering

ETERNAL Father, I offer You the most Precious Blood of Jesus Christ in atonement for my sins, in supplication for the holy souls in purgatory, and for the needs of holy Church.

Eternal Father, I offer You the most Precious Blood of Jesus with all its merits:

To expiate all the sins I have committed during all my life.

To purify the good I have done poorly during all my life.

To supply for the good I ought to have done, and that I have neglected all my life.

Prayer

ALMIGHTY and Eternal God, You have appointed Your only-begotten Son as the Redeemer of the world, and willed to be appeased by His Blood. Grant, we beg of You, that we may worthily adore this Price of our salvation, and through Its power be protected from the evils of this present life, so that we may rejoice in its fruits forever in heaven.

Lord Jesus Christ, You came down from heaven to earth from the bosom of the Father and shed Your Precious Blood for the remission of our sins. We humbly beg of You that in the day of judgment we, standing at Your right hand, may deserve to hear: "Come, you blessed," for You live and reign forever. Amen.

Litany

LORD, have mercy.
Christ, have mercy.
Lord, have mercy.
Christ, hear us.
Christ, graciously hear us.
God, the Father of Heaven, *have mercy on us.*
God, the Son, Redeemer of the world, *have mercy on us.*
God, the Holy Spirit, *have mercy on us.*
Holy Trinity, One God, *have mercy on us.*
Blood of Christ, only-begotten Son of the Eternal Father, *save us.**
Blood of Christ, Incarnate Word of God,
Blood of Christ, of the New and Eternal Testament,
Blood of Christ, falling upon the earth in the Agony,
Blood of Christ, shed profusely in the Scourging,
Blood of Christ, flowing forth in the Crowning with Thorns,
Blood of Christ, poured out on the Cross,
Blood of Christ, price of our salvation,
Blood of Christ, without which there is no forgiveness,
Blood of Christ, Eucharistic drink and refreshment of souls,
Blood of Christ, stream of mercy,
Blood of Christ, victor over demons,
Blood of Christ, courage of Martyrs,

* *Save us* is repeated after each invocation.

Blood of Christ, strength of Confessors,
Blood of Christ, bringing forth Virgins,
Blood of Christ, help of those in peril,
Blood of Christ, relief of the burdened,
Blood of Christ, solace in sorrow,
Blood of Christ, hope of the penitent,
Blood of Christ, consolation of the dying,
Blood of Christ, peace and tenderness of hearts,
Blood of Christ, pledge of eternal life,
Blood of Christ, freeing souls from purgatory,
Blood of Christ, most worthy of all honor,
Lamb of God, You take away the sins of the world: *spare us, O Lord.*
Lamb of God, You take away the sins of the world: *graciously hear us, O Lord.*
Lamb of God, You take away the sins of the world: *have mercy on us.*
℣. You have redeemed us, O Lord, in your Blood.
℟. *And made us, for our God, a kingdom.*

LET us pray. Almighty and Eternal God, You willed to honor the standard of the life-giving Cross by the Precious Blood of Your only-begotten Son. Grant, we beg You, that they who rejoice in honoring the same holy Cross and His Precious Blood may rejoice also in Your ever-present protection. We ask this through the same Christ our Lord. ℟. *Amen.*

—EASTER SEASON—

10. EASTER NOVENA

MEDITATION

THROUGH His Resurrection Jesus Christ was made known to us as God's Son in power, for He was obedient unto death and exalted as Lord of all. God chose His Son to be the one to suffer and to die for our sins. Because of His obedience He was raised up as Lord of all. By conquering death through His own power in His Resurrection, Jesus has shown Himself Master of life and death. Therefore He is true God and true Man, our Savior.

By His Death and Resurrection Jesus redeemed mankind from slavery to sin and to the devil. In obedience to His Father's Will He gave Himself for us in His Passion and arose from the dead that He might redeem us from sin and make us a people pleasing to the Father. He is the Messiah, God's own Son. He often said that what He was doing was done that the Scriptures might be fulfilled, because He saw His Father's Will in them.

We were slaves of the devil because of original sin and because of our personal sins. But Jesus made us free with the freedom of the children of God, for by His Resurrection He destroyed death and gave us the life of grace. Risen truly, the Lord gives us the Divine life of grace and pours out His Holy Spirit upon us.

Each of the Gospel episodes, as we read them during the Easter Season, centers on an all-important appearance to the Apostles in which they are commissioned for their future task, namely, to be witnesses of the Lord, Who is alive and will be with us until the end of the world (Mk 28:16-20). This is the Paschal message to all Christians.

Following the example of the Bible, Christians celebrate the mystery of our Lord's Resurrection for fifty days. The Lord's Ascension and Pentecost are the final memorial days. St. Paul says, "Christ, our Paschal Lamb, has been sacrificed; let us feast with joy" (1 Cor 5:6-8).

THE WORD OF GOD

"The Son of Man will be handed over to the chief priests and scribes, who will condemn Him to death. They will deliver Him to the Gentiles to be mocked and flogged and crucified. But on the third day He will be raised up."

—Mt 20:18-19

"In the time after His Suffering He showed Himself to [the Apostles] and gave many convincing proofs that He was alive. He appeared to them over the course of forty days and spoke to them about the Kingdom of God."

—Acts 1:3

"I handed on to you first of all what I myself received: that Christ died for our sins in accordance with the Scriptures; that He was buried; that He was raised on the third day in accordance with the Scriptures; that He was seen by Cephas, then by the Twelve. After that He was seen by five hundred brothers and sisters at once."

—1 Cor 15:3-5

NOVENA PRAYERS

Novena Prayer

JESUS, I believe that by Your own power You rose from death, as You promised, a glorious Victor. May this mystery strengthen my hope in another and better life after death, the resurrection of my body on the last day, and an eternity of happiness.

I firmly hope that You will keep Your promise to me and raise me up glorified. Through Your glorious Resurrection I hope that You will make my body like Your own in glory and life, and permit me to dwell with You in heaven for all eternity.

I believe that Your Resurrection is the crown of Your life and work as God-Man, because it is Your glorification. This is the beginning of the glorious life that was due to You as the Son of God. Your Resurrection is also the reward of Your life of suffering.

Jesus, my Risen Lord and King, I adore Your Sacred Humanity which receives this eternal

Kingdom of honor, power, joy, and glory. I rejoice with You, my Master, glorious, immortal, and all-powerful.

Through the glorious mystery of Your Resurrection I ask You to help me to rise with You spiritually and to live a life free from sin, that I may be bent upon doing God's will in all things, and may be patient in suffering. Through the Sacraments may my soul be enriched evermore with sanctifying grace, the source of Divine life. I also ask that You grant me this special request: *(Mention your request)*. May Your Will be done!

Prayer to the Risen Savior

JESUS, Son of God, I thank You for accepting the Cross and freeing us from the power of the enemy. I believe that by Your Resurrection You conquered the power of death and opened for us the way to eternal life.

I thank You for having redeemed me and for making me a child of God.

Look upon me with love. Raise me up and renew my life by the Spirit You have given me. May I follow You in Your risen life.

Draw me to the life where Your Spirit makes all life complete.

May I come at last to share the glory of Your Resurrection in heaven.

Prayer for Faith in the Risen Lord

FATHER in heaven, in the Resurrection of Your Son we come to know the full depth of Your love. You have freed us from the darkness of error and sin.

Increase my understanding and my love of the riches You have revealed in Him Who is Lord forever. May the light of faith shine in my words and actions. Help me to cling to Your truths with fidelity.

May I, who have received Your gift of faith, share in the new life of the Risen Christ. Keep me alive in Him, ever true to His teaching till Your glory is revealed in me.

Prayer

GOD our Father, by raising Christ Your Son You conquered the power of death and opened for us the way to eternal life. Let our celebration of Easter raise us up and renew our lives by the Spirit that is within us.

You wash away our sins in water, give us new birth in the Spirit, and redeem us in the Blood of Christ.

May we look forward with hope to our Resurrection, for You have made us Your sons and daughters and restored the joy of our youth.

We ask this through our Lord Jesus Christ, Your Son, Who lives and reigns with You and the Holy Spirit, one God, forever. Amen.

—ASCENSION—

11. ASCENSION NOVENA

MEDITATION

ON the fortieth day after His Resurrection, after having trained His Apostles for their high calling to establish the Kingdom of God on earth, Jesus prepared to ascend on high to where the glories of heaven awaited Him. He blessed His loving Mother and His Apostles and disciples and bade them farewell. A cloud received Him out of their sight.

The countless blessed spirits whom He had released from limbo accompanied Him as the first fruits of the redemption. All the hosts of heaven's Angels came out to meet Him, the Savior of the world.

As He took His place beside His heavenly Father, the whole court of heaven gave forth a glorious song of praise. It was the song heard by John in his visions: "Worthy is the Lamb That was slain to receive power and wealth, wisdom and might, honor and glory and praise!" (Rev 5:12).

Jesus ascended into heaven to enter into possession of His glory. While on earth He had always enjoyed the vision of God, but the glory of His Sacred Humanity had shone forth only at His Transfiguration. On His Ascension into heaven He took His place as Man beside His heavenly Father and was exalted above all other human creatures.

The night before He died Jesus prayed to His Father: "I have glorified You on earth by finishing the work You gave Me to do. Do You now, Father, glorify Me at Your side, with the glory I had in Your presence before the world began" (Jn 17:4-5).

Since His Humanity is united to the Divine Word, the second Person of the Blessed Trinity, It enjoys the right of eternal glory. It shares with the Father the infinite bliss and mighty power of God. This is the reward for all He has done and merited on earth. In heaven He is raised above all because on earth He has lowered Himself below all.

When the struggle of this life is over Jesus will give us the grace to share His joy and triumph in heaven for all eternity.

Jesus ascended into heaven to be our Mediator with His Father. There He is pleading for us. He ascended into heaven to give an account to His heavenly Father of the great work He had done on earth. The Church was born, grace springs up in abundance from His Cross of Calvary and is distributed through the Sacraments, God's justice is satisfied, hell and death are conquered, heaven is opened and man is saved. Jesus had a right to this glorious homecoming.

Christ's Ascension is also the assurance of our own ascension into heaven after the Last Judgment. He entered into His Kingdom to prepare a place for us, for He promised to come again to take us to Himself.

Let us ascend into heaven with Jesus in spirit there to dwell by faith, hope, and charity. Let us seek only the joys that are true!

THE WORD OF GOD

"After He had spoken to them, the Lord Jesus was taken up into heaven and took His seat at God's right hand." —Mk 16:19

"When He ascended on high, He took a host of captives and gave gifts to His people." —Eph 4:8

"If you have been raised with Christ, set your hearts on the things that are above, where Christ is seated at God's right hand. Be intent on things that are above rather than on things that are on earth." —Col 3:1-2

NOVENA PRAYERS

Novena Prayer

JESUS, I honor You on the feast of Your Ascension into heaven. I rejoice with all my heart at the glory into which You entered to reign as King of heaven and earth. When the struggle of this life is over, give me the grace to share Your joy and triumph in heaven for all eternity.

I believe that You entered into Your glorious Kingdom to prepare a place for me, for You promised to come again to take me to Yourself. Grant that I may seek only the joys of Your friendship and love, so that I may deserve to be united with You in heaven.

In the hour of my own homecoming, when I appear before Your Father to give an account of my life on earth, have mercy on me.

Jesus, in Your love for me You have brought me from evil to good and from misery to happiness. Give me the grace to rise above my human weakness. May Your Humanity give me courage in my weakness and free me from my sins.

Through Your grace give me the courage of perseverance, for You have called and justified me by faith. May I hold fast to the life You have given me and come to the eternal gifts You promised.

You love me, dear Jesus. Help me to love You in return. I ask You to grant this special favor: *(Mention your request).*

By Your unceasing care, guide my steps toward the life of glory You have prepared for those who love You. Make me grow in holiness and thank You by a life of faithful service.

Prayer of Praise to Jesus in Glory

I PRAISE You, dearest Heart of Jesus, Fountain of all goodness.

I praise You, most kind Heart of Jesus, for the boundless graces that have flowed and shall continue to flow from You into the souls of the just.

I praise You, most gentle Heart of Jesus, for the tender love with which You have so often refreshed devout hearts through Divine consolations.

I praise You, most loving Heart of Jesus, for the fullness of Your grace, the splendor of Your virtues, the generosity of Your Heart, and the purity of Your love.

I praise You, royal Heart of Jesus, for Your victory over death and sin, Your power over souls, and Your triumph over the living and the dead.

I praise You, Heart so poor and yet so rich, for having despised all earthly riches and for having renounced all earthly honors.

I praise You, most obedient Heart of Jesus, that hungered after the fulfillment of the Divine Will and thirsted after the greater glory of God and the salvation of souls.

I praise You, most generous Heart of Jesus, that did not seek Its own glory; most patient Heart, that willingly bore the greatest insults; most unselfish Heart, that longed for and lovingly embraced the Cross.

Most Sacred Heart of Jesus, teach me to love You with my whole heart, and grant that, according to the little strength I have, I may imitate Your wonderful virtues. Amen.

Prayer

GOD our Father, make us joyful in the Ascension of Your Son Jesus Christ. May we follow Him into the new creation, for His Ascension is our glory and our hope. We ask this through our Lord Jesus Christ, Your Son, Who lives and reigns with You and the Holy Spirit, one God, forever. Amen.

—CORPUS CHRISTI—

12. SACRAMENT OF THE HOLY EUCHARIST

MEDITATION

THE Eucharist is the Sacrament which contains the true Body and Blood of Jesus Christ, together with His Soul and Divinity, the entire living and glorified Christ, under the appearances of bread and wine.

The Council of Trent clearly defines the truth that is the very foundation of all Christ-life and worship: "In the Most Holy Sacrament of the Eucharist there is contained truly, really, and substantially, the Body and Blood of our Lord Jesus Christ, together with His Soul and Divinity, indeed the whole Christ."

As Catholics we believe that Jesus Christ remains personally present on the altar as long as there is a consecrated Host in the tabernacle. He is the same Jesus Christ, true God and true Man, Who walked the streets of Galilee and Judea. We believe that He actually comes as our personal guest every time we receive Holy Communion.

The Eucharist is one of the seven Sacraments instituted by Christ to give us a share in the life of God. It is the greatest of all seven Sacraments since It contains Christ Himself, the Divine Author of the Sacraments.

There are three different aspects or phases of the Eucharist. The first is called the Real Presence of Christ on the altar while there remains a consecrated Host in the tabernacle. The second phase of the Eucharist is the Sacrifice of the Mass, and the third is Holy Communion.

The word "Eucharist," from the Greek, means "Thanksgiving." It is applied to this Sacrament because our Lord gave thanks to His Father when He instituted It, and also because the Holy Sacrifice of the Mass is the best means of expressing our thanks to God for His favors.

The Holy Eucharist is the very center of Catholic worship, the heart of Catholic life. Because the Church believes that the Son of God is truly present in the Blessed Sacrament, she erects beautiful churches and adorns them richly.

The Sacrifice of the Mass is not only a ritual which reminds us of the sacrifice of Calvary. In it, through the ministry of priests, Christ continues till the end of time the sacrifice of the Cross in an unbloody manner.

The Eucharist is also a meal which reminds us of the Last Supper, celebrates our unity together in Christ, and already now makes present the Messianic banquet of the Kingdom of heaven.

In the Eucharist Jesus nourishes Christians with His own Self, the Bread of Life, so that they may become a people more pleasing to God and filled with greater love of God and neighbor.

The Eucharist is reserved in our churches to be a powerful help to prayer and the service of others. Reservation of the Blessed Sacrament means that at the end of Communion the remaining Consecrated Bread is placed in the tabernacle and reverently reserved. The Eucharist reserved is a continuing sign of our Lord's real presence among His people and spiritual food for the sick and dying.

We owe gratitude, adoration, and devotion to the Real Presence of Christ in the Blessed Sacrament reserved. We show this devotion in our visits to the tabernacle in our churches and in Benediction when the Blessed Sacrament is exposed to the people for reverence and adoration and the priest blesses the people with the Lord's Body.

The tombs of the Martyrs, the paintings on the walls in the catacombs, and the custom of reserving the Blessed Sacrament in the homes of the first Christians in the years of persecution show the unity of faith in the first centuries of Christianity in the doctrine that in the Eucharist Christ is really contained, offered, and received. From the Eucharist the entire Church drew strength for courageous struggles and brilliant victories.

The Eucharist is the center of all Sacramental life because it is of the greatest importance for uniting and strengthening the Church.

The Novena in honor of the Sacrament of the Holy Eucharist can be made many times during the Liturgical Year to deepen our faith in this great mystery of love, the center of all Sacramental life of the Church.

THE WORD OF GOD

"I am the Bread of life. Your ancestors ate the manna in the wilderness, and yet they died. This is the Bread that comes down from heaven so that one may eat it and never die. I Myself am the living Bread come down from heaven. Whoever eats this Bread will live forever; and the Bread I will give is My Flesh, for the life of the world. . . .

"Unless you eat the Flesh of the Son of Man and drink His Blood, you do not have life within you. Whoever eats My Flesh and drinks My Blood has eternal life, and I will raise him up on the last day. For My Flesh is real food and My Blood is real drink.

"Whoever eats My Flesh and drinks My Blood dwells in Me, and I in him. Just as the living Father sent Me and I have life because of the Father, so whoever eats Me will have life because of Me." —Jn 6:48-57

"Jesus took bread, and after He had pronounced the blessing, He broke it and gave it to His disciples, saying, 'Take this and eat; this is My Body.' Then He took a cup, and after offering thanks He gave it to them, saying, 'Drink from this, all of you. For this is My Blood of the Covenant, which will be shed on behalf of many for the forgiveness of sins.' " —Mt 26:26-28

"Do this in memory of Me." —Lk 22:19

NOVENA PRAYERS

Novena Prayer

I THANK You, Jesus, my Divine Redeemer, for coming upon the earth for our sake, and for instituting the adorable Sacrament of the Holy

Eucharist in order to remain with us until the end of the world. I thank You for hiding beneath the Eucharistic species Your infinite majesty and beauty, which Your Angels delight to behold, so that I might have courage to approach the throne of Your mercy.

I thank You, most loving Jesus, for having made Yourself my food, and for uniting me to Yourself with so much love in this wonderful Sacrament that I may live in You.

I thank You, my Jesus, for giving Yourself to me in this Blessed Sacrament, and so enriching it with the treasures of Your love that You have no greater gift to give me. I thank You not only for becoming my food but also for offering Yourself as a continual Sacrifice to Your Eternal Father for my salvation.

I thank You, Divine Priest, for offering Yourself as a Sacrifice daily upon our altars in adoration and homage to the Most Blessed Trinity, and for making amends for our poor and miserable adorations. I thank You for renewing in this daily Sacrifice the actual Sacrifice of the Cross offered on Calvary, in which You satisfy Divine justice for us poor sinners.

I thank You, dear Jesus, for having become the priceless Victim to merit for me the fullness of heavenly favors. Awaken in me such confidence in You that their fullness may descend ever more fruitfully upon my soul. I thank You for offering Yourself in thanksgiving to God for all His benefits, spiritual and temporal, which He has bestowed upon me.

In union with Your offering of Yourself to Your Father in the Holy Sacrifice of the Mass, I ask for this special favor: *(Mention your request).*

If it be Your holy Will, grant my request. Through You I also hope to receive the grace of perseverance in Your love and faithful service, a holy death, and a happy eternity with You in heaven. Amen.

Prayer to Christ the High Priest

LORD Jesus Christ, our great High Priest, by Your Death and Resurrection You revealed Yourself as the mediating Lamb of Sacrifice between the Father and ourselves. You call us to share Your dying and rising in the Sacraments of Baptism and Confirmation so that we might unite ourselves in offering Your sacrifice through Your Priesthood in the Eucharist, thus entering into Your Kingdom on earth by becoming Your Holy People.

Lord Jesus Christ, our great High Priest, grant to us Your Spirit of Love and Life which unites us to Yourself as Victim and Priest so that God's plan of salvation for all people is established within us.

Lord Jesus Christ, our great High Priest, grant to us Your Spirit of Wisdom and Unity which makes us all one in Your Mystical Body, the Church, so that we may be Your witnesses in this world.

Lord Jesus Christ, our great High Priest, heal us by Your Cross, renew us by Your Resurrection, sanctify us by Your Holy Spirit, glorify us by Your Kingship, redeem us by Your Priesthood, so that we may be one in You as You are one with Your Father in the Holy Spirit.

Lord Jesus, gather us all into Your Person—Victim, Priest, King—by the saving Eucharistic Meal You and we offer on the Altar of Sacrifice now and all of our pilgrim days on earth. Then when we are called into Your Kingdom in heaven, may we share with all the Saints the glory of Your love and life which is Yours with the Father and the Holy Spirit for all ages to come without end. Amen.

Prayer

O LORD, You have given us this Sacred Banquet, in which Christ is received, the memory of His Passion is renewed, the mind is filled with grace, and a pledge of future glory is given to us

℣. You have given them bread from heaven.

℟. *Containing in itself all sweetness.*

LET us pray. God our Father, for Your glory and our salvation You appointed Jesus Christ eternal High Priest. May the people He gained for You by His Blood come to share in the power of His Cross and Resurrection by celebrating His Memorial in this Eucharist, for He lives and reigns with You and the Holy Spirit, one God, forever. Amen.

O Jesus, since You have left us a remembrance of Your Passion beneath the veils of this Sacrament, grant us, we pray, so to venerate the sacred mysteries of Your Body and Blood that we may always enjoy the fruits of Your Redemption, for You live and reign forever. ℟. *Amen.*

13. NOVENA OF HOLY COMMUNIONS

MEDITATION

THE Sacrifice of the Mass is not only a ritual which reminds us of the sacrifice of Calvary. In it, through the ministry of priests, Christ continues till the end of time the Sacrifice of the Cross in an unbloody manner.

The Eucharist is also a meal which reminds us of the Last Supper, celebrates our unity together in Christ, and already now makes present the Messianic banquet of the Kingdom of Heaven.

Jesus nourishes our soul with Himself, the Bread of Life. He offered Himself as a sacrifice on the Cross. In Holy Communion we partake of the Body that was given in death for us and the Blood that was shed for our salvation. This holy meal reminds us of what happened at the Last Supper when Jesus told His Apostles to do this in memory of Him.

The Communion of the Mass is the meal of the Lord's Body that nourishes us with the life of God and unites us to Jesus and to one another. In drawing us to union with Jesus, our heavenly Father draws us closer to each other because we share in the Divine life of Jesus through His grace. The Holy Eucharist is not only a sign of the unity and love that binds us to Jesus and each other, but it gives us the grace we need to make that love strong and sincere.

Holy Communion is already giving us a part of the banquet of Christ in the Kingdom of Heaven because it is the same Son of God made Man who will be united with us in a union of joy forever in heaven. Jesus also promised that our body would some day enjoy His presence. He said, "Whoever eats My Flesh and drinks My Blood has eternal life, and I will raise him up on the last day" (Jn 6:54). The meal, prepared for us by God the Father, makes us ready to take part in that heavenly communion with Jesus and His Father.

In the Eucharist Jesus nourishes Christians with His own Self, the Bread of Life, so that they may become a people more pleasing to God and filled with greater love of God and neighbor.

Holy Communion is Jesus Christ Himself under the appearances of bread and wine uniting Himself to the Christian to nourish his soul. He said, "I am the living Bread That came down from heaven. Whoever eats this Bread will live forever; and the bread that I will give is My Flesh, for the life of the world" (Jn 6:51).

Holy Communion helps us to love God more because of the Divine grace which grows in our souls. This same grace helps us to love others for the love of God. Jesus strengthens us through actual or sacramental grace that we may overcome temptation and avoid sinning against God and our neighbor. Only by the help of His grace can we truly live a life of charity and fulfill His greatest commandment.

Therefore, the Eucharist is a Sacrament of unity because it unites the faithful more closely with God and with one another. By eating the Body of the Lord, we are taken up into a close union with Him and one another. St. Paul said, "Because there is one loaf of bread we who are many are one body, for we all partake of the one loaf" (1 Cor 10:17).

The following suggestions about the Novena of Holy Communions may be useful: (1) Receive Holy Communion nine days in succession or on nine Sundays in petition for a special favor. Omitting one or more days of the Novena in no way affects the fruitfulness of the Novena. The power of the Novena is based on our Lord's words: "If you abide in Me and My words abide in you, you may ask for whatever you wish, and it will be done for you" (Jn 15:7). "Whoever eats My Flesh and drinks My Blood dwells in Me, and I dwell in him" (Jn 6:56).

(2) After you have made your novena of *petition* for a special favor, make another immediately in *thanksgiving*, even if you have not received the favor you prayed for. The Novena of Holy Communions is meant to be like a perpetual novena. It is a sacramental novena. The Eucharist is the richest source of grace, and the Mass is the highest form of worship.

Your prayers at Holy Communion were answered—perhaps not in your way, but in God's way; and He knows best! You have done our Lord's Will, for He said at the Last Supper, "Take this and eat; this is My Body. . . . Drink from this, all of you. For this is My Blood of the Covenant, which will be shed on behalf of many for the forgiveness of sins" (Mt 26:26-27). You have also fulfilled the wish of the Church.

THE WORD OF GOD

"I am the Vine, you are the branches. Whoever abides in Me, and I in him, will bear much fruit. Apart from Me you can do nothing." —Jn 15:5

"Amen, amen, I say to you, unless you eat the Flesh of the Son of Man and drink His Blood, you do not have life in you." —Jn 6:53

"Now it is no longer I who live, but it is Christ Who lives in me. The life I live now in the body I live by faith in the Son of God Who loved me and gave Himself up for me." —Gal 2:20

"Where your treasure is, there will your heart also be." —Lk 12:34

NOVENA PRAYERS

Novena Prayer

JESUS, my Eucharistic Friend, accept this Novena of Holy Communions which I am making in order to draw closer to Your Sacred Heart in sincerest love. If it be Your holy Will, grant the special favor for which I am making this novena: *(Mention your request).*

Jesus, You have said, "Ask and you shall receive; seek and you shall find; knock and it shall be opened to you" (Mt 7:7). Through the intercession of Your most holy Mother, Our Lady of the Blessed Sacrament, I ask, I seek, I knock; please grant my prayer.

Jesus, You have said, "If you ask the Father for anything in My Name, He will give it to you" (Jn 16:23). Through the intercession of Your most holy Mother, Our Lady of the Blessed Sacrament, I ask the Father in Your Name to grant my prayer.

Jesus, You have said, "Whatever you ask in My Name I will do" (Jn 14:13). Through the intercession of Your most holy Mother, Our Lady of the Blessed Sacrament, I ask in Your Name to grant my prayer.

Jesus, You have said, "If you abide in Me, and My words abide in you, you may ask for whatever you wish, and it will be done for you" (Jn 15:7). Through the intercession of Your most holy Mother, Our Lady of the Blessed Sacrament, may my request be granted, for I wish to live in You through frequent Holy Communion.

Lord, I believe that I can do nothing better in order to obtain the favor I desire than to attend Holy Mass and to unite myself in Holy Communion most intimately with You, the Source of all graces. When You are really and truly present in my soul as God and Man, my confidence is greatest, for You *want* to help me, because You are all-good; You *know how* to help me, because You are all-wise; You *can* help me, because You are all-powerful. Most Sacred Heart of Jesus, I believe in Your love for me!

Jesus, as a proof of my sincerest gratitude, I promise to receive You in Holy Communion as often as I am able to do so—at every Mass I attend, if possible. Help me to love You in the Holy Eucharist as my greatest Treasure upon earth. May the effects of frequent Holy Communion help me to serve You faithfully so that I may save my soul and be with You forever in heaven. Amen.

Hymn—Adoro Te

HIDDEN God, devoutly I adore You,
Truly present underneath these veils:
All my heart subdues itself before You,
Since it all before You faints and fails.

Not to sight, or taste, or touch be credit,
Hearing only do we trust secure;
I believe, for God the Son has said it—
Word of Truth that ever shall endure.

On the cross was veiled Your Godhead's splendor,
Here Your Manhood lies hidden too;
Unto both alike my faith I render,
And, as sued the contrite thief, I sue.

Though I look not on Your wounds with Thomas,
You, my Lord, and You, my God, I call:
Make me more and more believe Your promise,
Hope in You, and love You over all.

O memorial of my Savior dying,
Living Bread, that gives life to man;
Make my soul, its life from You supplying,
Taste Your sweetness, as on earth it can.

Deign, O Jesus, Pelican of heaven,
Me, a sinner, in Your Blood to lave,
To a single drop of which is given
All the world from all its sin to save.

Contemplating, Lord, Your hidden presence,
Grant me what I thirst for and implore,
In the revelation of Your essence
To behold Your glory evermore.

Saint Thomas Aquinas

For Frequent Communicants

LOVING Jesus, You came into the world to give to all souls Your Divine life. To preserve and strengthen this supernatural life and to sustain us against our daily weaknesses and shortcomings, You wished to become our daily Food.

Humbly we beg You, pour forth Your Divine Spirit upon us through the love of Your Sacred Heart. May the souls who, through the misfortune of sin, have lost the life of grace, return once more to You.

Let those who share Your Divine life come to Your Holy Table frequently, that by partaking of this Holy Banquet, they may receive the strength to be victorious in the daily struggle with sin and thus grow ever purer and holier in Your sight, till they come to eternal life with You. Amen.

Our Lady of the Blessed Sacrament

VIRGIN Mary, Our Lady of the most Blessed Sacrament, glory of the Christian people, joy of the Universal Church, salvation of the whole world, pray for us and grant to all the faithful true devotion to the most Holy Eucharist, that they may become worthy to receive it daily.

Prayer

SACRED Banquet, in which Christ is received, the memory of His Passion is renewed, the mind is filled with grace, and a pledge of future glory is given to us.

℣. You have given them bread from heaven.

℟. *Containing in itself all sweetness.*

LET us pray. God, since You have left us a remembrance of Your Passion beneath the veils of this Sacrament, grant us, we pray, so to venerate the sacred Mysteries of Your Body and Blood that we may always enjoy the fruits of Your Redemption. You live and reign forever. ℟. *Amen.*

—SACRED HEART OF JESUS—

14. SACRED HEART OF JESUS

MEDITATION

DEVOTION to the Sacred Heart, as we know it, began about the year 1672. On repeated occasions, Jesus appeared to Saint Margaret Mary Alacoque, a Visitation nun, in France, and during these apparitions He explained to her the devotion to His Sacred Heart as He wanted people to practice it. He asked to be honored in the symbol of His Heart of flesh; he asked for acts of reparation, for frequent Communion, Communion on the First Friday of the month, and the keeping of the Holy Hour.

When the Catholic Church approved the devotion to the Sacred Heart of Jesus, she did not base her action only on the visions of Saint Margaret Mary. The Church approved the devotion on its own merits.

There is only one Person in Jesus, and that Person was at the same time God and Man. His Heart, too, is Divine—it is the Heart of God.

There are two things that must always be found together in the devotion to the Sacred Heart: Christ's Heart of flesh and Christ's love for us. True devotion to the Sacred Heart means devotion to the Divine Heart of Christ insofar as His Heart represents and recalls His love for us.

In honoring the Heart of Christ, our homage lingers on the Person of Jesus in the fullness of His love. This love of Christ for us was the moving force of all He did and suffered for us—in Nazareth, on the Cross, in giving Himself in the Blessed Sacrament, in His teaching and healing, in His praying and working. When we speak of the Sacred Heart, we mean Jesus showing us His Heart, Jesus all love for us and all lovable.

Jesus Christ is the incarnation of God's infinite love. The Human Nature which the Son of God took upon Himself was filled with love and kindness that has never found an equal. He is the perfect model of love of God and neighbor.

Every day of His life was filled with repeated proofs of "Christ's love that surpasses all knowledge" (Eph 3:19). Jesus handed down for all time the fundamental feature of His character: "Take My yoke upon you and learn from Me, for I am meek and humble of Heart" (Mt 11:29). He invited all, refusing none, surprising friends and rivals by His unconditional generosity.

The meaning of love in the life of Jesus was especially evident in His sufferings. Out of love for His Father He willed to undergo the death of the Cross. "The world must come to understand that I love the Father and that I do just as the Father has commanded Me" (Jn 14:31).

The love that Jesus bore toward us also urged Him to undergo the death of the Cross. At the Last

Supper, He said,"No one can have greater love than to lay down his life for his friends" (Jn 15:13).

What enhances Christ's love is the sovereign liberty with which He offered Himself. He said,"This is why the Father loves Me, because I lay down My life in order to take it up again. No one takes it away from Me. I lay it down of My own free will. And as I have the right to lay it down, I have the power to take it up again. This command I have received from My Father" (Jn 10:17-18).

Jesus loved people because they belonged to His Father. Before He died He prayed, "It is for them I pray. I do not pray for the world, but for those You gave Me because they are Yours" (Jn 17:9). He did mankind much good for God's sake, seeing in every person a child of God and the image of His Father.

He loved people for His own sake, because they were really so much in need of help, and because He wished to win them over to His teaching by His innumerable favors.

When we see Jesus lavishly offering inexhaustible treasures of compassion and mercy, we are able to conceive something of the immensity of that ocean of Divine kindness and love from which the Sacred Heart draws these treasures for us.

The Heart of Jesus never ceases to love us in heaven. He sanctifies us through the Sacraments. These are inexhaustible fountains of grace and holiness which have their source in the boundless ocean of the Sacred Heart of Jesus.

The Solemnity of the Sacred Heart of Jesus is celebrated on the Friday following the Second Sunday after Pentecost.

THE WORD OF GOD

"This is the Covenant that I will make with the house of Israel after those days, says the Lord. I will put My law within them, and I will inscribe it upon their hearts; I will be their God, and they shall be My people." —Jer 31:33

"Take My yoke upon you and learn from Me, for I am meek and humble of Heart." —Mt 11:28

"I have come to spread fire on the earth, and how I wish it were already blazing!" —Lk 12:49

"When they came to Jesus and saw that He was already dead, they did not break His legs but one of the soldiers thrust a lance into His side, and immediately a flow of Blood and water came forth." —Jn 19:33-34

NOVENA PRAYERS

Novena Prayer

DIVINE Jesus, You have said, "Ask and you shall receive; seek and you shall find; knock and it shall be opened to you." Behold me kneeling at Your feet, filled with a lively faith and confidence in the promises dictated by Your Sacred Heart to St. Margaret Mary. I come to ask this favor: *(Mention your request)*.

To whom can I turn if not to You, Whose Heart is the source of all graces and merits? Where should I seek if not in the treasure which contains all the riches of Your kindness and mercy? Where should I knock if not at the door through which God gives Himself to us and through which we go to God? I have recourse to You, Heart of Jesus. In You I find consolation when afflicted, protection when persecuted, strength when burdened with trials, and light in doubt and darkness.

Dear Jesus, I firmly believe that You can grant me the grace I implore, even though it should require a miracle. You have only to will it and my prayer will be granted. I admit that I am most unworthy of Your favors, but this is not a reason for me to be discouraged. You are the God of mercy, and You will not refuse a contrite heart. Cast upon me a look of mercy, I beg of You, and Your kind Heart will find in my miseries and weakness a reason for granting my prayer.

Sacred Heart, whatever may be Your decision with regard to my request, I will never stop adoring, loving, praising, and serving You. My Jesus, be pleased to accept this my act of perfect resignation to the decrees of Your adorable Heart, which I sincerely desire may be fulfilled in and by me and all Your creatures forever.

Grant me the grace for which I humbly implore You through the Immaculate Heart of Your most sorrowful Mother. You entrusted me to her as her child, and her prayers are all-powerful with You. Amen.

Memorare

REMEMBER, most kind Jesus, that no one was ever abandoned who had recourse to Your Sacred Heart, implored Its help, or called for mercy. Filled with this confidence, Divine

Heart, ruler of all hearts, I come to You, oppressed beneath the weight of my sins. Do not reject my poor prayers, but listen to them mercifully, and be pleased to answer them.

Prayer

MOST holy Heart of Jesus, fountain of every blessing, I adore You, I love You, and with a lively sorrow for my sins, I offer myself to You.

Make me humble, patient, pure, and obedient to Your Will. Grant, dear Jesus, that I may live in You and for You. Protect me in the midst of danger; comfort me in my afflictions; give me health of body, assistance in my temporal needs, your blessing on all that I do, and the grace of a holy death.

Love of the Heart of Jesus, inflame my heart.

Charity of the Heart of Jesus, flow into my heart.

Strength of the Heart of Jesus, support my heart.

Mercy of the Heart of Jesus, pardon my heart.

Patience of the Heart of Jesus, grow not weary of my heart.

Kingdom of the Heart of Jesus, be in my heart.

Wisdom of the Heart of Jesus, teach my heart.

Will of the Heart of Jesus, guide my heart.

Zeal of the Heart of Jesus, consume my heart.

Immaculate Virgin Mary, pray for me to the Sacred Heart of Jesus.

For the Salvation of Souls

MOST Holy Heart of Jesus, shower Your blessings abundantly upon Your holy Church, upon the Supreme Pontiff, and upon all the clergy and religious.

Grant perseverance to the just, convert sinners, and enlighten unbelievers. Bless my relatives, friends, and benefactors. Assist the dying, deliver the holy souls in purgatory, and extend over all hearts the gentle empire of Your love.

To You, most merciful Heart of Jesus, I commend all these souls, and in their behalf I offer to You all Your merits in union with the merits of Your most blessed Mother and of all the Angels and Saints, together with all the Masses, Communions, prayers, and good works which are being offered this day throughout Christendom.

Prayer to Answer Christ's Love

I LOOK upon Your Heart, dear Lord, filled with love for us. Because of Your love, forgive my sins. I have wounded Your Heart, but You bring me forgiveness and grace. Help me to prove my grateful love and make amends for my sins.

I thank You for the gifts of love I have received from Your Sacred Heart. Open my heart to share Your life and continue to bless me with Your love.

Make me strong in faith and bring me to the glory You promise through the merits of the Passion and Death You accepted for love of me. Through Your Resurrection, may I love You for all eternity in Your heavenly Kingdom.

Offering

MY God, I offer You all my prayers, works, joys, and sufferings in union with the Sacred Heart of Jesus, for the intentions for which He pleads and offers Himself in the Holy Sacrifice of the Mass, in thanksgiving for Your favors, in reparation for my sins, and in humble supplication for my temporal and eternal welfare, for the needs of our holy Mother the Church, for the conversion of sinners, and for the relief of the poor souls in purgatory.

Act of Consecration

I (N.), give and consecrate to the Sacred Heart of our Lord Jesus Christ, my person, my life, my actions, my pains and sufferings, so that I may no longer be willing to use any part of my being except to honor, love, and glorify the Sacred Heart.

It is my unchanging intention to be all His and to do all for love of Him. I renounce at the same time with all my heart whatever can displease Him.

I, therefore, take You, Sacred Heart, for the only object of my love, the protector of my life, the pledge of my salvation, the remedy of my weakness and inconstancy, the atonement for the faults of my life, and the secure refuge at the hour of my death.

Be then, Heart of goodness, my justification before God the Father, and turn away from me the punishment of His just anger. Heart of love, I put my confidence in You, because I fear everything from my own sinfulness and weakness. I hope for all things from Your mercy and generosity.

Destroy in me all that can displease or resist Your holy Will. Let Your pure love impress You so deeply upon my heart that I may never forget You or be separated from You. May my name, by Your loving kindness, be written in You, because in You I desire to place all my happiness and all my glory in living and dying in very bondage to You. *(Saint Margaret Mary Alacoque)*

Litany of the Sacred Heart of Jesus

LORD, have mercy.
Christ, have mercy.
Lord, have mercy.
Christ, hear us.
Christ, graciously hear us.
God the Father of heaven, *have mercy on us.*

God the Son, Redeemer of the world, *have mercy on us.*
God the Holy Spirit,*
Holy Trinity, one God,
Heart of Jesus, Son of the Eternal Father,
Heart of Jesus, formed by the Holy Spirit in the womb of the Virgin Mother,
Heart of Jesus, substantially united to the Word of God,
Heart of Jesus, of infinite majesty,
Heart of Jesus, sacred temple of God,
Heart of Jesus, tabernacle of the Most High,
Heart of Jesus, house of God and gate of heaven,
Heart of Jesus, burning furnace of charity,
Heart of Jesus, abode of justice and love,
Heart of Jesus, full of goodness and love,
Heart of Jesus, abyss of all virtues.
Heart of Jesus, most worthy of all praise,
Heart of Jesus, king and center of all hearts,
Heart of Jesus, in Whom are all the treasures of wisdom and knowledge,
Heart of Jesus, in Whom dwells the fullness of Divinity,
Heart of Jesus, in Whom the Father was well pleased,
Heart of Jesus, of Whose fullness we have all received,
Heart of Jesus, desire of the everlasting hills,
Heart of Jesus, patient and most merciful,
Heart of Jesus, enriching all who invoke You,

* Have mercy on us *is repeated after each invocation.*

Heart of Jesus, fountain of life and holiness,
Heart of Jesus, propitiation for our sins,
Heart of Jesus, loaded down with opprobrium,
Heart of Jesus, bruised for our offenses,
Heart of Jesus, obedient to death,
Heart of Jesus, pierced with a lance,
Heart of Jesus, source of all consolation,
Heart of Jesus, our life and resurrection,
Heart of Jesus, our peace and reconciliation,
Heart of Jesus, victim for our sin,
Heart of Jesus, salvation of those who trust in You,
Heart of Jesus, hope of those who die in You,
Heart of Jesus, delight of all the Saints,
Lamb of God, You take away the sins of the world; *spare us, O Lord.*
Lamb of God, You take away the sins of the world; *graciously hear us, O Lord.*
Lamb of God, You take away the sins of the world; *have mercy on us.*

℣. Jesus meek and humble of heart.
℟. *Make our hearts like Yours.*

LET us pray. Almighty and Eternal God, look upon the Heart of Your most beloved Son, and upon the praises and satisfaction which He offers You in the name of sinners; and to those who implore Your mercy, in Your great goodness, grant forgiveness in the Name of the same Jesus Christ, Your Son, Who lives and reigns with You, forever and ever. ℟. *Amen.*

—CHRIST THE KING—

15. CHRIST THE KING

MEDITATION

JESUS began his public life by announcing His Kingdom. "The Kingdom of God is at hand! Reform your lives and believe in the Gospel!" (Mk 1:14).

The Kingdom of God is primarily spiritual. Its final realization consists in the union of all the blessed in the possession of God in heaven.

Entrance into this Kingdom comes through the acceptance of the Gospel message by faith and the receiving of Baptism. Jesus said to His Apostles, "Go forth into every part of the world and proclaim the Gospel to all creation. Whoever believes and is baptized will be saved; whoever does not believe will be condemned" (Mk 16:15-16).

To belong to the Kingdom of God, then, demands that a person be born again of God. He becomes a child of God, not merely by external adoption, but by a real and true sharing of the Divine life. "To those who did accept Him and who believed in His Name He granted power to become children of God" (Jn 1:12).

Christ's kingdom is not a kingdom of earth. He said to Pilate, "My Kingdom does not belong to this world" (Jn 18:36).

The name by which the Kingdom of God is most commonly called is the Church. It is at once Divine and human; on earth and in heaven. Small as a mustard seed in its beginning, it was destined to become catholic, that is, to embrace all the earth. This concept of the Church as the one universal Kingdom of God makes it evident that there can be only one true Church, just as there can be only one true Kingdom of God.

The Church is Jesus Christ, living on and acting in the world through His duly authorized ministers, until the end of time. He gave to His Church a form, an organization which would enable it to carry on His work on earth—to teach, to rule, and to administer to the souls of men.

Membership in the Kingdom of God is the most precious thing that a person can possess. We must regard it as a pearl beyond price and gratefully sacrifice for this gift.

Jesus Christ is *our King*. He is the Firstborn of all creation because He is before all—all things have been created in Him, through Him, and for Him. He is the most excellent of all creatures as well as their Creator because He is the perfect image of God, the firstborn in the order of creation.

Christ is the center of all God's saving works because the Christian can fulfill his task of making creation give glory to God through the power of Jesus, the Risen Savior.

Jesus said to Pilate, "My Kingdom does not belong to this world. . . . It is you who say that I am a King. For this was I born, and for this I came into the world: to testify to the truth. Everyone who is devoted to the truth listens to My voice" (Jn 18:36-37).

It is of faith that Jesus Christ, as Man, has the fullest spiritual power, leading to salvation, establishing the Church and her Sacraments, and disposing of all graces in the supernatural order. In virtue of the union of His human nature with the Divine, He possesses still greater power, which is the foundation of His Kingship.

We, as individuals, must strive to be subject to Christ the King most perfectly, in mind, will, and heart, because we were purchased at the price of His own Precious Blood. Christ must be King of the home and all human society.

Jesus asks us to believe in Him and put our hope in Him for the future, and to love Him with all our heart. He said, "The Father loves the Son and He has entrusted everything into His hand. Whoever believes in the Son has eternal life" (Jn 3:35-36).

THE WORD OF GOD

"I Myself have anointed My King on Zion, My holy mountain. . . . You are My Son; this day I have begotten You. Simply make the request of Me, and I will give You the nations as Your inheritance, and the ends of the earth as Your possession. You will rule them." —Ps 2:6-9

"The Lord God will give Him the throne of His ancestor David. He will rule over the house of Jacob forever, and of His Kingdom there will be no end." —Lk 1:32-33

" 'My Kingdom does not belong to this world.' . . . Pilate then said to Him, 'So you are a King?' Jesus answered, 'It is you who say that I am a King. For this was I born, and for this I came into the world: to testify to the truth.' "

—Jn 18:36-39

"On His robe and on His thigh He has a Name inscribed: 'King of kings and Lord of lords.' "

—Rev 19:16

NOVENA PRAYERS

Novena Prayer

JESUS, You declared that Your Kingdom is upon the earth, but not of the earth; it is a spiritual, supernatural Kingdom, the Kingdom of truth. It fights with the power of conviction, and conquers by this means the hearts that by right belong to it. You Yourself are witness to this truth, and You Yourself are the Truth.

Jesus, I believe that You are truly a King because You have come into the world to institute among people the rule of God; every person who is of the truth, who believes in God and recognizes His authority in human affairs, owes You a loyal and undivided allegiance and "hears Your voice."

As a Catholic I am a member of Your Kingdom, and You are my King. To You I owe loyalty, obedience, and love. Help me to carry out these most sacred duties toward You. I wish to be "of the truth," that is, "a child of God," and gladly to hear Your voice and follow You in all things. I accept You as my King and submit to Your authority.

Reign supremely in my heart and in my life. Your reign is heavenly peace; Your law is love. Help me to pray and work that Your Kingdom may come into every soul, every family, every nation.

Jesus, since I honor You as my King, I come to You with great confidence, asking You to grant this special favor, if it be Your holy Will: *(Mention your request).*

Lord Jesus Christ, my King, I adore You as the Son of God, and through the prayers of Your most loving Mother I beg of You, send me from out of the abundance of Your loving Heart the grace of the Holy Spirit in order that He may enlighten my ignorance, purify and sanctify my sinful heart, and confirm me in Your holy love. This I request through the love of the Father and the Holy Spirit, through Your infinite mercy, and through the merits of all Your Saints. Amen.

Consecration

CHRIST, Jesus, I acknowledge You as King of the universe. All that has been made has been created for You. Make full use of Your rights over me.

I renew the promises I made in Baptism when I renounced Satan and all his pomps and works. I promise to live a good Christian life. Especially, I undertake to help, to the extent of my means, to secure the triumph of the rights of God and of Your Church.

Divine Heart of Jesus, I offer You my poor efforts so that all hearts may acknowledge Your sacred Royalty and the Kingdom of Your peace may be established throughout the entire universe. Amen.

Prayer

ALMIGHTY and merciful God, you break the power of evil and make all things new in Your Son Jesus Christ, the King of the universe. May all in heaven and on earth acclaim Your glory and never cease to praise You.

Father all-powerful, God of love, You have raised our Lord Jesus Christ from death to life, resplendent in glory as King of creation. Open our hearts; free all the world to rejoice in His peace, to glory in His justice, and to live in His love. Bring all mankind together in Jesus Christ Your Son Whose Kingdom is with You and the Holy Spirit, one God, forever. Amen.

Preface

FATHER, all-powerful and ever-living God, we do well always and everywhere to give You thanks.

You anointed Jesus Christ, Your only Son, with the oil of gladness, as the Eternal Priest and Universal King. As Priest He offered His life on the altar of the Cross and redeemed the human race by this one perfect sacrifice of peace.

As King He claims dominion over all creation, that He may present to You, His almighty Father, an eternal and universal Kingdom: a Kingdom of truth and life, a Kingdom of holiness and grace, a Kingdom of justice, love, and peace.

And so, with all the choirs of Angels in heaven we proclaim Your glory and join in their unending hymn of praise.

God the Holy Spirit

—PENTECOST—

16. THE HOLY SPIRIT

MEDITATION

THE Holy Spirit is God, and Third Person of the Holy Trinity, really God, the same as the Father and the Son are really God. He is the love of the Father and the Son.

Christ promised that this Spirit of Truth would come and would remain within us. "I will ask the Father and He will give you another Advocate—to dwell with you always: the Spirit of truth, Whom the world cannot accept, since it neither sees Him nor knows Him; but you will know Him because He dwells with you and will be in you" (Jn 14:16-17).

The Holy Spirit came at Pentecost, never to depart. Fifty days after Easter, on Pentecost Sunday, He changed the Apostles from weak fearful men to brave men of faith that Christ needed to spread His Gospel to the nations.

The Holy Spirit is present in a special way in the Church, the community of those who believe in Christ as Lord. He helps the Church to continue the work of Christ in the world. By His presence people are moved by His grace to unite themselves with God and men in sincere love and to fulfill their duties to God and man. He makes the Church pleasing to God because of the Divine life of grace which He gives. By the power of the Gospel He makes the Church grow. He renews it with His gifts, and leads it to perfect union with Jesus.

The Holy Spirit guides the Pope, bishops, and priests of the Church in their work of teaching Christ's doctrine, guiding souls, and giving God's grace to the people through the Sacraments. He directs all the work of Christ in the Church—the care of the sick, the teaching of children, the guidance of youth, the comforting of the sorrowful, the support of the needy.

We should honor the Holy Spirit by loving Him as our God and by letting Him guide us in life. St. Paul reminds us to do so. "Do you not know that you are the temple of God, and that the Spirit of God dwells in you?" (1 Cor 3:16).

Since the Holy Spirit is always with us if we are in the state of grace, we should often ask Him for the light and strength we need to live a holy life and to save our soul. (The universal symbol of the Holy Spirit is a *dove*.)

THE WORD OF GOD

"Amen, amen, I say to you, no one can enter into the Kingdom of God unless he is born of water and the Spirit. Flesh begets flesh, Spirit begets spirit." —Jn 3:5-6

"These things I have told you while I am still with you. The Advocate, the Holy Spirit Whom the Father will send in My Name, will instruct you in everything, and bring to your mind all that I told you." —Jn 14:25-26

"When the days of Pentecost were drawing to a close, they were all together in one place. Suddenly, there came a sound from heaven as of a strong, driving wind, and it filled the whole house where they were sitting. They saw what appeared to be tongues of fire that separated and settled upon each of them. They were all filled with the Holy Spirit and began to speak in foreign tongues as the Spirit enabled them to do." —Acts 2:1-4

"To each person the manifestation of the Spirit is given for the common good. To one through the Spirit is given the message of wisdom, to another the message of knowledge by means of the same Spirit, to another faith by the same Spirit, to another gifts of healing by that same Spirit, to another the working of miracles, to another prophecy, to another the discernment of spirits, to another speaking in tongues, and to still another the interpretation of tongues. But all these are the work of one and the same Spirit, Who allots to everyone according as He wills." —1 Cor 12:7-11

NOVENA PRAYERS

Novena Prayer

HOLY Spirit, third Person of the Blessed Trinity, Spirit of truth, love, and holiness, proceeding from the Father and the Son, and equal to Them in all things, I adore You and love You with all my heart.

Dearest Holy Spirit, confiding in Your deep, personal love for me, I am making this novena for the following request, if it should be Your holy Will to grant it: *(Mention your request).*

Teach me, Divine Spirit, to know and seek my last end; grant me the holy fear of God; grant me true contrition and patience. Do not let me fall into sin. Give me an increase of faith, hope, and charity, and bring forth in my soul all the virtues proper to my state of life.

Make me a faithful disciple of Jesus and an obedient child of the Church. Give me efficacious grace sufficient to keep the Commandments and to receive the Sacraments worthily. Give me the four Cardinal Virtues, Your Seven Gifts, Your Twelve Fruits. Raise me to perfection in the state of life to which You have called me and lead me through a happy death to everlasting life. I ask this through Christ our Lord. Amen.

Consecration

HOLY Spirit, Divine Spirit of light and love, I consecrate to You my understanding, heart, and will, my whole being, for time and for eternity. May my understanding be always submissive to Your heavenly inspirations and to the teaching of the Catholic Church, of which You are the infallible Guide. May my heart be ever inflamed with the love of God and of my neighbor. May my will be ever conformed to the Divine Will. May my whole life be faithful to the imitation of the life and virtues of our Lord and Savior Jesus Christ, to Whom with the Father and You be honor and glory forever.

God, Holy Spirit, Infinite Love of the Father and the Son, through the pure hands of Mary, Your Immaculate Spouse, I place myself this day, and all the days of my life, upon Your chosen altar, the Divine Heart of Jesus, as a sacrifice to You, consuming fire, being firmly resolved now more than ever to hear Your voice and to do in all things Your most holy and adorable Will.

For the Seven Gifts of the Holy Spirit

BLESSED Spirit of *Wisdom,* help me to seek God. Make Him the center of my life and order my life to Him, so that love and harmony may reign in my soul.

Blessed Spirit of *Understanding,* enlighten my mind, that I may know and love the truths of faith and make them truly my own.

Blessed Spirit of *Counsel,* enlighten and guide me in all my ways, that I may always know and do Your holy Will. Make me prudent and courageous.

Blessed Spirit of *Fortitude,* uphold my soul in every time of trouble or adversity. Make me loyal and confident.

Blessed Spirit of *Knowledge,* help me to know good from evil. Teach me to do what is right in the sight of God. Give me clear vision and firmness in decision.

Blessed Spirit of *Piety*, possess my heart, incline it to a true faith in You, to a holy love of You, my God, that with my whole soul I may seek You, Who are my Father, and find You, my best, my truest joy.

Blessed Spirit of *Holy Fear*, penetrate my inmost heart that I may ever be mindful of Your presence. Make me fly from sin, and give me intense reverence for God and for my fellow men who are made in God's image.

Prayer

GRANT, we beg of You, Almighty God, that we may so please Your Holy Spirit by our earnest prayers, that we may, by His grace, be freed from all temptations and merit to receive the forgiveness of our sins. Through Christ our Lord. Amen.

Come, Holy Spirit, Creator Blest!

COME, Holy Spirit, Creator blest!
And in our souls take up Your rest;
Come, with Your grace and heavenly aid,
To fill the hearts which You have made.

O Comforter, to You do we cry,
O heavenly Gift of God Most High;
O Fount of life and Fire of love,
And sweet Anointing from above!

You in Your sevenfold Gifts are known;
You, Finger of God's hand, we own;
You, Promise of the Father, You,
Who do the tongue with power imbue.

Kindle our senses from above
And make our hearts o'erflow with love;
With patience firm and virtue high,
The weakness of our flesh supply.

Far from us drive the foe we dread,
And grant us Your true peace instead;
So shall we not, with You for Guide,
Turn from the path of life aside.

Oh, may Your grace on us bestow
The Father and the Son to know;
And You, through endless times confessed,
Of both the eternal Spirit blest.

Now to the Father and the Son,
Who rose from death, be glory given,
With you, O holy Comforter,
Henceforth by all in earth and heaven. Amen.

℣. Send forth Your Spirit and they shall be created;

℟. *And You shall renew the face of the earth.*

LET us pray. God, You have taught the hearts of Your faithful people by sending them the light of Your Holy Spirit. Grant us by the same Spirit to have a right judgment in all things and evermore to rejoice in His holy comfort. Through Christ our Lord. ℟. *Amen.*

The Holy Trinity

17. HOLY TRINITY

MEDITATION

THE mystery of the Trinity is the one true God in three Persons—the Father, the Son, and the Holy Spirit.

The mystery of the Trinity was expressed in the Person, words, and actions of Jesus Christ. After speaking through the Prophets, God sent His Son. He came among people in the Person of His Son, Jesus Christ. Jesus told us the "Good News" of salvation. This message is found in the New Testament. By His words and actions, and especially in His holy Person, Jesus made known the deepest truths about God. The Blessed Trinity is the deepest of all mysteries.

Jesus has revealed to us the secrets of the Kingdom of Heaven. The greatest of His teachings is the secret of God Himself. He has told us of the life of God. He taught us that in the one God there are three Persons, each equal to each other. He told us the names of these three Divine Persons: Father, Son, and Holy Spirit.

Jesus Christ revealed *Himself* as the eternal and Divine Son of God. He said that He is the Son, the only-begotten Son of the Father, equal to the Father.

Jesus more fully revealed *the Father*. He constantly spoke of His Father, calling Him always by that name. He taught us to love our heavenly Father because He loves us and wants to help us in all the needs of our body and soul. He wants to bring His children to His heavenly home.

Jesus revealed the third Divine Person, *the Holy Spirit,* whom the Father and He, as the Risen Lord, sent to His Church. Jesus promised to send a third Divine Person, the equal of Himself and the Father.

Jesus, the Divine Teacher, taught His disciples about the true God and called them to become sons of God through the gift of the Spirit.

We honor the Blessed Trinity by trying to remember the presence of God the Father, Son, and Holy Spirit in our soul and to understand, as much as we can through faith, that through Baptism we are called to a close union of love with the three Divine Persons.

THE WORD OF GOD

"Oh, the depth of the riches and wisdom and knowledge of God! How inscrutable are His judgments and how unfathomable His ways! 'For who has known the mind of the Lord or who has been His counselor? Or who has given Him anything in order to receive a gift in return?' For from Him and through Him and for Him are all things. To Him be glory forever. Amen." —Rom 11:33-36

"There are three that bear witness in heaven: the Father, the Word, and the Holy Spirit; and these three are one."
—1 Jn 5:7 (Vulgate)

"There are different varieties of gifts but the same Spirit. There are different kinds of service but the same Lord. There are different forms of activities but the same God Who produces all of them in everyone."
—1 Cor 12:4-5

NOVENA PRAYERS

Novena Prayer

GOD Eternal *Father,* bless me through the love with which You have begotten Your only Son from all eternity and shared with Him the fullness of Your own Divinity.

Bless me through the love which has made us children of adoption and partakers of the treasures of Your Divinity.

Bless me through the love with which You have sent us Your Son and the Holy Spirit in order to work the miracles of Your power and mercy in us. Grant that I may always revere and honor You as my great God and love You with my whole heart as the best of fathers.

Eternal Father, grant my petition: *(Mention your favor).*

God Eternal *Son,* image of the splendor of the heavenly Father, bless me through the love with which You surround us, Your poor creatures. You have become our Brother according to the flesh to make us Your brothers according to Your Divinity, and an image of Your splendor.

Bless me through the marvelous goodness of Your Sacred Heart which caused You to choose death in order to bring us life.

Bless me through the love with which You always plead for us in the Blessed Sacrament and at the throne of God and give Yourself to us in Holy Communion. Grant that all this love and all Your bitter pain may not be lost on me.

Eternal *Son*, grant my petition: *(Mention your favor).*

God *Holy Spirit*, mutual Love of the Father and the Son, bless me through the love with which You proceed from the Father and the Son and unite Them in eternal unity.

Bless me through the love with which You give Yourself to us as our greatest Gift, dispensing Your Divine graces to us and transforming sinners into children of God.

Bless me through the love with which You dwell in the Sacred Heart of Jesus, through Whose merits the earth is filled with grace and made a dwelling place for the God of heaven. Grant that I, Your faithful servant, may always allow myself to be led by You so as to advance in virtue and reach eternal happiness.

God Holy Spirit, grant my petition: *(Mention your favor).*

Offering

MOST Holy Trinity, Godhead indivisible, Father, Son, and Holy Spirit, our first beginning and our last end, You have made us after Your own image and likeness. Grant that all the thoughts of my mind, all the words of my mouth, all the affections of my heart and all my actions may be always conformed to Your most holy Will. After having seen You here below in Your manifestations and in a dark manner by faith, may I come at last to see You face to face in the perfect possession of You forever in heaven. Amen.

Prayer

ALMIGHTY and Everlasting God, You have given us, Your servants, grace by the profession of the true faith to acknowledge the glory of the Eternal Trinity, and in the power of Your Divine Majesty to worship the Unity. We beg You to grant that, by our fidelity in this same faith, we may always be defended from all dangers. Through Christ our Lord. Amen.

Praise and Worship

I PRAISE You, Father all-powerful. I praise You, Divine Son, our Lord and Savior. I praise You, Spirit of love.

One God, three Persons, be near me in the temple of my soul. You reveal Yourself in the depths of my being. Draw me to share in Your life and love.

Your power is beyond all words to describe, Your glory is measureless, Your mercy is without limits, Your love for mankind is beyond all telling. Look down upon me and in Your kindness grant to me the riches of Your compassion and mercy, a share in Your Divine life.

May I come to live more fully the life I profess and come to the glory of Your Kingdom.

Te Deum—Hymn of Thanksgiving

O GOD, we praise You, and acknowledge You to be the supreme Lord.
Everlasting Father, all the earth worships You.
All the angels, the heavens and all angelic powers,
All the cherubim and seraphim, continually cry to You:
Holy, holy, holy, Lord God of Hosts!
Heaven and earth are full of the majesty of Your glory.
The glorious choir of the Apostles,
The wonderful company of Prophets,
The white-robed army of martyrs, praise You.

Holy Church throughout the world acknowledges you:
The Father of infinite majesty;
Your adorable, true and only Son;
Also the Holy Spirit, the Comforter!

O Christ, You are the King of glory!
You are the everlasting Son of the Father.
When You took it upon Yourself to deliver man,
You did not disdain the Virgin's womb.
Having overcome the sting of death, You opened the Kingdom of Heaven to all believers.

You sit at the right hand of God in the glory of the Father.

We believe that You will come to be our Judge.

We, therefore, beg You to help Your servants whom You have redeemed with Your Precious Blood.

Let them be numbered with Your Saints in everlasting glory.

Save Your people, O Lord, and bless Your inheritance!

Govern them, and raise them up forever.

Every day we thank You.

And we praise Your Name forever; yes, forever and ever.

O Lord, deign to keep us from sin this day.

Have mercy on us, O Lord, have mercy on us.

Let your mercy, O Lord, be upon us, for we have hoped in You.

O Lord, in You I have put my trust; let me never be put to shame.

"Hail, holy Queen, Mother of Mercy . . . to you do we send up our sighs, mourning and weeping."

Part Two
THE BLESSED VIRGIN MARY

—JANUARY—

18. MARY, THE MOTHER OF GOD

(January 1)

MEDITATION

THE most sublime of Mary's privileges is her Divine Maternity. Without that Maternity, her other privileges would not exist; she herself would not exist, for she was created only to be the Mother of God.

Mary's Divine Maternity is great also because this privilege is the reason for her other privileges—her Immaculate Conception, miraculous virginity, fullness of grace, Assumption, and the spiritual maternity of all mankind. The Divine Maternity explains everything in her; without this Maternity nothing in Mary can be explained.

In her teaching concerning the union of the human and the Divine natures in Christ the Church states that Jesus Christ is God and Man, perfect God and perfect Man, and that this Divinity and Humanity are united in only one Person so that the actions of the Divine Nature or the Human Nature are the actions of one person, the Divine Person.

Since God was born of Mary, she is the Mother of God. If we could not say that she is the Mother of God for having given a body to the Son of God, then neither could we adore this Body; nor would we have been redeemed by the sacrifice of this Body on the Cross; nor would we be united to the Divinity in receiving this Body in the Eucharist.

Mary's Divine Maternity is such a sublime privilege that no creature, not even Mary herself, can understand it fully. To understand her dignity as Mother of God in all its fullness, we would have to understand fully the dignity of the Son of God whose Mother she is.

The dignity of the Divine Maternity raises Mary above all the rest of creation. As Mother of God she surpasses, in an immeasurable degree, all other creatures, Angels, and human beings. They are God's servants, but she is His Mother.

We have the sublime dignity of being children of God by adoption; Jesus alone is His Son by nature. But Mary is not the adoptive Mother of the Son of God; she is His real Mother. We can lose our Divine adoption, but Mary can never lose her Divine Maternity. God might have created a more beautiful world, more perfect people, more marvelous spirits; He could not have made anything more wonderful than a Mother of God.

Mary's Divine Maternity places her in a very wonderful relationship with the three Divine

Persons. She is the loving daughter of the Father, because, before all creatures, she was predestined to be His daughter at the same moment that He decreed the Incarnation of His Son. He bestowed marvelous privileges upon her and loved her more than all other creatures together. As Mother of the Son of God, she is associated with the Father in the generation of His Son as man. With the Father she, too, can say: "This is my beloved Son in Whom I am well pleased."

Mary is the Mother of the Son of God. She fulfills the duties and enjoys the rights of a true mother. From her own flesh and blood, she formed the Body of her Son. She nourished Him, clothed Him, educated Him. She commanded Him and He obeyed. How can we ever understand the great love that bound their hearts together!

Mary is the spouse of the Holy Spirit because according to the Gospel and the teaching of the Apostles' Creed, she conceived of the Holy Spirit the Son of God, made Man. She is also called the temple of the Holy Spirit because, in virtue of her Immaculate Conception and her fullness of grace, He dwells within her in a most singular manner.

During all eternity it will be one of our greatest joys to admire the infinite love of God for Mary whose Son He willed to be, just as He is in all truth the Son of the Father. The Divine Maternity itself, more than any particular privilege, is a mark of God's unequalled love for Mary. We should rejoice with her in the happiness that filled her heart because of such love. We can ask Mary to pray to God that we return His love with some of the generosity and fervor with which she loved Him.

THE WORD OF GOD

"When the fullness of time had come, God sent His Son born of a woman ... so that we might receive our adoption as children." —Gal 4:4-5

"Shout for joy,... O daughter of Jerusalem!... The King of Israel, the Lord, is in your midst." —Zep 3:14-15

"The Word became flesh and dwelt among us. And we saw His glory: the glory of the Only-begotten of the Father, full of grace and truth." —Jn 1:14

"[Mary] brought forth her firstborn Son and wrapped Him in swaddling clothes and laid Him in a manger." —Lk 2:7

NOVENA PRAYERS

Novena Prayer

I GREET you, ever-blessed Virgin, Mother of God, throne of grace, miracle of almighty power! I greet you, sanctuary of the Most Holy Trinity and Queen of the Universe, Mother of mercy and refuge of sinners!

Most loving Mother, attracted by your beauty and sweetness, and by your tender compassion, I confidently turn to you, and beg of you to obtain for me of your dear Son the favor I request in this novena: *(Mention your request).*

Obtain for me also, Queen of Heaven, the most lively contrition for my many sins and the grace to imitate closely those virtues which you practiced so faithfully, especially humility, purity, and obedience. Above all, I beg you to be my mother and protectress, to receive me into the number of your devoted children, and to guide me from your high throne of glory.

Do not reject my petitions, Mother of mercy! Have pity on me, and do not abandon me during life or at the moment of my death.

Daughter of the Eternal Father, Mother of the Eternal Son, Spouse of the Holy Spirit, Temple of the Adorable Trinity, pray for me. Immaculate and tender Heart of Mary, refuge of the needy and hope of sinners, filled with the most lively respect, love, and gratitude, I devote myself forever to your service, and I offer you my heart with all that I am and all that is mine.

Accept this offering, sweet Queen of Heaven and Earth, and obtain for me of your dear Son, Jesus Christ, the favors I ask through your intercession in this novena. Obtain for me also a generous, constant love of God, perfect submission to His holy Will, the true spirit of a Christian, and the grace of final perseverance. Amen.

Memorare

REMEMBER, O most gracious Virgin Mary, that never was it known that anyone who fled to your protection, implored your help, or sought your intercession, was left unaided. Inspired with this confidence I fly to you, O Virgin of virgins, my Mother. To you I come; before you I stand, sinful and sorrowful. O Mother of the Word Incarnate, despise not my petitions, but in your mercy hear and answer me. Amen.

Consecration

HOLIEST Virgin, with all my heart I venerate you above all the Angels and Saints in paradise as the Daughter of the Eternal Father, and I consecrate to you my soul with all its powers. *Hail Mary, etc.*

Holiest Virgin, with all my heart I venerate you above all the Angels and Saints in paradise as the Mother of the only-begotten Son, and I consecrate to you my body with all its senses. *Hail Mary, etc.*

Holiest Virgin, with all my heart I venerate you above all the Angels and Saints in paradise as the beloved Spouse of the Holy Spirit, and I consecrate to you my heart and all its affections, praying you to obtain for me from the Most Holy Trinity all the graces I need for my salvation. *Hail Mary, etc.*

Litany

LORD, have mercy.
Christ, have mercy.
Lord, have mercy.
Christ, hear us.
Christ, graciously hear us.

God the Father of heaven, *have mercy on us.*

God the Son, Redeemer of the world, *have mercy on us.*

God the Holy Spirit, *have mercy on us.*
Holy Trinity, one God, *have mercy on us.*
Holy Mary, *pray for us.*
Holy Mother of God,*
Holy Virgin of virgins,
Mother of Christ,
Mother of the Church,
Mother of Divine grace,
Mother most pure,
Mother most chaste,
Mother inviolate,
Mother undefiled,
Mother most amiable,
Mother most admirable,
Mother of good counsel,
Mother of our Creator,
Mother of our Savior,
Virgin most prudent,
Virgin most venerable,
Virgin most renowned,
Virgin most powerful,
Virgin most merciful,
Virgin most faithful,
Mirror of justice,
Seat of wisdom,
Cause of our joy,
Spiritual vessel,
Vessel of honor,
Singular vessel of devotion,
Mystical rose,
Tower of David,
Tower of ivory,
House of gold,
Ark of the covenant,
Gate of heaven,
Morning star,
Health of the sick,
Refuge of sinners,
Comforter of the afflicted,
Help of Christians,
Queen of angels,
Queen of patriarchs,
Queen of prophets,
Queen of apostles,
Queen of martyrs,
Queen of confessors,
Queen of virgins,
Queen of all saints,
Queen conceived without original sin,
Queen assumed into heaven,
Queen of the most holy Rosary,
Queen of families,
Queen of peace,

Lamb of God, You take away the sins of the world; *spare us, O Lord.*

**Pray for us* is said after every invocation.

Lamb of God, You take away the sins of the world;
graciously hear us, O Lord.

Lamb of God, You take away the sins of the world;
have mercy on us.

℣. Pray for us, O Holy Mother of God,

℟. *That we may be made worthy of the promises of Christ.*

LET us pray. Grant, we beg You, O Lord God, that we Your servants may enjoy lasting health of mind and body, and by the glorious intercession of the Blessed Mary ever Virgin, be delivered from present sorrow and enter into the joy of eternal happiness. Through Christ our Lord. ℟. *Amen.*

19. OUR LADY OF PERPETUAL HELP

MEDITATION

THE miraculous picture of Madonna and Child rests on the main altar of the church of the Redemptorist Fathers in Rome. It was first in the possession of a wealthy Cretan merchant, then brought to Rome and eventually enthroned in St. Matthew's Church. For three hundred years crowds of pilgrims have journeyed far to see this picture, the source of many cures. In 1812, St. Matthew's Church was razed, and for fifty-four years the picture's location was not known. When it was found, Pope Pius IX gave it to the Redemptorist Fathers for their church on the spot where Mary first had been revered in this special manner as Our Lady of Perpetual Help.

The miraculous picture is painted like an icon. Two Angels designated as Sts. Michael and Gabriel are seen beside the Virgin's head, carrying in their veiled hands the instruments of Christ's Passion, the

Cross, the spear, and the sponge. The picture was probably painted by a Greek artist of the thirteenth or fourteenth century.

Mary is invoked as Our Lady of Perpetual Help because she affords help to Christians even in all temporal needs. Although she is now enthroned in heaven, she still takes an interest in our misery and relieves our wants.

Mary brings us help especially in our spiritual needs. She is a most merciful Mother who rejects no sinner. She lovingly interests herself in our behalf and tries to reconcile us to her Son when we have sinned. She assists us in temptation. She confirms us in good and obtains for us the grace of making progress in the path of virtue, for she desires nothing more ardently than that we all become partakers of the fruits of redemption, won for us by her Son. In our efforts to reach holiness, she supports us and obtains for us the grace of perseverance. We can ask nothing of her that will give her greater pleasure or that she will grant more willingly than the grace to do good.

Above all, Mary will assist us in the hour of death, which is a crucial moment in our life because it is then that we prepare for the judgment. As the exalted Queen of Heaven she takes the souls of her faithful servants under her protecting mantle, accompanies them to the judgment seat of her Son, and there she becomes their intercessor.

Mary is still the Mother of God in heaven as she was on earth; Jesus, Who is omnipotence itself, remains her Son for all eternity. Her love for us is now even more intense and more compassionate, because she knows our misery better in heaven. She obtains gentle rest for all who are laden with trouble and pain; she gives comfort to the afflicted and healing to the sick.

Mary is our Mother of Perpetual Help, and therefore we should have an unbounded confidence in her. She can help us, for her prayer is all-powerful with God, and she will help us, for she is our Mother and she loves us as her children.

THE WORD OF GOD

"Can a woman forget her infant and be without tenderness for the child of her womb? Yet even if she should forget, I will never forget you." —Isa 49:15

"The wine ran out, and the Mother of Jesus ... said to the attendants, 'Do whatever He tells you.' " —Jn 2:3-5

"Blessed are they who watch daily at my gates ... for those who find me find life and shall have salvation from the Lord." —Prov 8:34-35

NOVENA PRAYERS

Novena Prayer

MOTHER of Perpetual Help, behold at your feet a sinner who has recourse to you and has confidence in you. Mother of mercy, have pity on me. I hear all calling you the refuge and hope of sinners. Be, then, my refuge and my hope. For the love of Jesus Christ, your Son, help me.

Give your hand to a poor sinner who commends himself to you and dedicates himself to your lasting service. I praise and thank God

Who in His mercy has given to me this confidence in you, a sure pledge of my eternal salvation.

It is true that in the past, I, miserable and wretched, have fallen into sin because I did not have recourse to you. But I know that with your help I shall be able to overcome myself. I know, too, that you will help me, if I commend myself to you. But I fear that in the occasions of sin, I may neglect to call upon you and thus run the risk of being lost.

This grace, then, I seek of you; for this I implore you as much as I know how and as much as I can: that in all the attacks of hell I may ever have recourse to you and say to you: "O Mary, help me. O Mother of Perpetual Help, do not let me lose my God." *3 Hail Marys.*

Mother of Perpetual Help, aid me ever to call upon your powerful name, since your name is the help of the living and the salvation of the dying. Mary most pure, Mary most sweet, grant that your name from this day forth may be to me the very breath of life. Dear Lady, do not delay in coming to help me when I call upon you, for in all the temptations that trouble me, in all the needs of my life, I will ever call upon you, repeating: "Mary, Mary."

What comfort, what sweetness, what confidence, what consolation fills my soul at the sound of your name, at the very thought of you! I give thanks to our Lord, Who for my sake has given you a name so sweet, so lovable and so mighty. But I am not content only to speak your name; I will call upon you because I love you. I want that love to remind me always to call you Mother of Perpetual Help.

3 Hail Marys.

Mother of Perpetual Help, you are the dispenser of every grace that God grants us in our misery. For this reason He has made you so powerful, so rich, and so kind that you might help us in our needs. You are the advocate of the most wretched and abandoned sinners, if they but come to you. Come to my aid, for I commend myself to you.

In your hands I place my eternal salvation; to you I entrust my soul. Count me among your most faithful servants. Take me under your protection; that is enough for me. If you protect me, I shall fear nothing. I shall not fear my sins, because you will obtain for me their pardon and remission. Neither shall I fear the evil spirits, because you are mightier than all the powers of hell.

I fear only that through my own negligence I may forget to recommend myself to you and so lose my soul. My dear Lady, obtain for me the forgiveness of my sins, love for Jesus, final perseverance, and the grace to have recourse to you at all times, Mother of Perpetual Help.

3 Hail Marys.

(Saint Alphonsus Liguori)

—FEBRUARY—

20. OUR LADY OF LOURDES AND BERNADETTE

(February 11)

MEDITATION

BETWEEN February 11 and July 16, 1858, the Blessed Virgin came down from heaven eighteen times and showed herself at Lourdes to Bernadette Soubirous a little girl of fourteen years of age. On February 11, while gathering wood, Bernadette heard a whistle of wind. With astonished eyes she saw a niche in the upper part of a rock filled with golden light, and there in the midst of it stood a Lady of great beauty.

Her robe glowed with the whiteness of snow in the sunshine and swept in majestic folds to the ground. Her head and shoulders were framed by a white veil, which fell the full length of her robe. A blue sash encircled her waist, and its two ends, wide and unornamented, reached down in front almost to her feet. Each of her feet bore a rose of purest gold. A rosary, whose beads were white and whose cross and chain were of gold, hung from her right arm. Her hands were open, and her arms outstretched slightly in front.

In her apparitions our Lady appealed for penance and prayers for sinners. On March 25, the feast of the Annunciation, the Blessed Mother declared her name to Bernadette and to the world. On that day Bernadette made this request: "My Lady, would you be so kind as to tell me who you are?"

This is how Bernadette describes what happened in that last apparition: "Three times I asked the Apparition her name. At the third instance, she stretched out her hands, which until then she held joined, raised them, and she said: 'I am the Immaculate Conception.' "Then having completed her great message to the world, the Lady smiled on Bernadette and withdrew without further word of farewell.

Less than four years before these apparitions, on December 8, 1854, Pope Pius IX proclaimed that Mary in the first instant of her conception was preserved free from all stain of original sin through the merits of her Divine Son. At Lourdes the Virgin Mary had come to confirm the infallible utterance of God's Vicar on earth and declared herself not only immaculately conceived, but "the Immaculate Conception."

On October 30, 1867, Bernadette made her religious profession in the Convent of the Congregation of the Sisters of Nevers, France. In January, 1873, Bernadette became ill.

On April 16, about three in the afternoon, Bernadette prayed: "Holy Mary, Mother of God, pray for me, a poor sinner!" She made a Sign of the Cross, took the glass that was handed to her, twice swallowed a few drops of water, and then bending her head gently gave up her soul to her Creator.

Bernadette died, worn out with physical suffering, on April 16, 1879, at the age of thirty-six. Now her incorrupt body can be seen as she lay in death in the side chapel of the motherhouse of the Sisters of Charity at Nevers, where she lived and died as Sister Marie Bernard. Thirty years after her death her body was found in a perfect state of preservation, undoubtedly a token of love of the Immaculate Virgin Mary. She was beatified in 1925, and on December 8, 1933, she was canonized by Pope Pius XI. Her feast day is February 18.

THE WORD OF GOD

"You have visited the earth and make it overflow; you enrich it greatly." —Ps 65:10

"I have chosen and sanctified this place that my name may be there forever, and my eyes and my heart may be there perpetually." —2 Chr 7:16

"I found delight in the human race." —Prov 8:31

NOVENA PRAYERS

Novena Prayer

MARY, Mother of God, I firmly believe in the doctrine of Holy Mother Church concerning your Immaculate Conception: namely, that you were, in the first instant of your conception, by the singular grace and privilege of God, in view of the merits of Jesus Christ, the Savior of the human race, preserved immune from all stain of original sin.

Alone of all the children of Adam, you were gifted with the fullness of sanctifying grace that made you the object of a very special love on the part of God. How wonderful were the workings of Divine power to make you a fitting dwelling for the Redeemer of the world! With no tendency to evil, but with a deep yearning for the highest virtue, you glorified God more than all His other creatures. At the very instant of your conception your mind was filled with the light of God, and your will was entirely conformed to the Divine Will. You were always intimately united with God.

I thank God with you for these wonderful blessings. Help me to imitate your holiness to some degree. Your holiness was not the result of the privilege of your Immaculate Conception and sanctifying grace alone, but followed from your gift of yourself to God and your constant cooperation with His graces. Help me to be generous with God by turning to good account the graces that He ever bestows on me, and by rising promptly when I fall, with renewed confidence in His mercy.

Ever Immaculate Virgin, Mother of mercy, health of the sick, refuge of sinners, comfort of the afflicted, you know my wants, my troubles, my sufferings. Deign to cast upon me a look of mercy.

By appearing in the Grotto of Lourdes, you were pleased to make it a privileged sanctuary, from which you dispense your favors; and already many sufferers have obtained the cure of their infirmities, both spiritual and corporal. I come, therefore, with the most unbounded confidence to implore your maternal intercession.

Obtain, O loving Mother, the granting of my requests. Through gratitude for your favors, I will endeavor to imitate your virtues that I may one day share your glory.

Through your loving compassion shown to thousands of pilgrims who come to your shrine at Lourdes, and through your special love for your devoted client Bernadette, I ask for this grace if it be the Will of God: *(Mention your request).*

Our Lady of Lourdes, aid me through your prayer with your Divine Son, to be a true child of yours, as Bernadette was, and to grow daily into your likeness.

Prayer to Saint Bernadette

SAINT Bernadette, little shepherdess of Lourdes, favored with eighteen apparitions of the Immaculate Virgin Mary and with the privilege of lovingly conversing with her, now that you are eternally enjoying the entrancing beauty of the Immaculate Mother of God, do not forsake me, your devoted client, who am still in this valley of tears.

Intercede for me that I, too, may walk the simple paths of faith. Help me to imitate your example, at our heavenly Queen's request, by saying the Rosary daily and by doing penance for sinners.

Teach me to imitate your wonderful devotedness to God and our Lady, the Immaculate Conception, so that, like you, I may be blessed with the grace of lasting faithfulness and enjoy the happiness in heaven of the eternal vision of God the Father, Son, and Holy Spirit. Amen.

Prayer

GOD of infinite mercy, we celebrate the feast of Mary, Our Lady of Lourdes, the sinless Mother of God. May her prayers help us to rise above our human weakness. We ask this through our Lord Jesus Christ, Your Son Who lives and reigns with You and the Holy Spirit, one God, forever. Amen.

—JUNE—

21. THE IMMACULATE HEART OF MARY

(Sat. following 2nd Sun. after Pentecost)

MEDITATION

ANY form of veneration of the Blessed Virgin is always directed to her person. So, too, in venerating the Immaculate Heart of Mary, we revere not only the real physical Heart of our Blessed Mother, but also her person as the source and bearer of all her virtues. We expressly honor her Heart as a symbol of her love for God and for people.

The first impulses to the veneration of the Immaculate Heart of Mary are found in Holy Scripture. After the arrival of the shepherds to the crib we read: "Mary kept in mind all these things, pondering them in her heart" (Lk 2: 19).

After Mary and Joseph found the twelve-year-old Jesus in the Temple, Scripture says: "He went down with them and came to Nazareth, and was obedient to them. And His Mother kept all these things carefully in her Heart" (Lk 2:51).

At the presentation of Jesus in the Temple, Simeon predicted: "And your own soul a sword shall pierce" (Lk 2:35). These words were verified beneath the Cross, for as the Heart of Jesus was pierced by a lance, the Heart of His Blessed Mother was transfixed by the sword of sorrow. The Heart of Jesus had its first beat in the shelter of the most pure Heart of His Mother Mary, and this most pure Heart had also received in spirit the last beat of the Heart of Jesus. If the Sacred Heart would not be without the loving Heart of His Mother in heaven, He did not wish to be honored apart from her upon earth.

In one of the first apparitions at Fatima in 1917, our Lady said that Lucy must remain on earth a while longer to spread devotion to the Immaculate Heart of Mary.

In the third apparition at Fatima, July 13, 1917, our Lady told Lucy: "Our Lord wishes that devotion to my Immaculate Heart be established in the world. If what I tell you is done, many souls will be saved and there will be peace; the war will end. . . . I ask the consecration of Russia to my Immaculate Heart and Communion of reparation on the First Saturday of each month. . . . If my requests are granted, Russia will be converted and there will be peace. . . . In the end my Immaculate Heart will triumph, and an era of peace will be conceded to humanity."

On October 31, 1942, Pope Pius XII consecrated the world to the Immaculate Heart of Mary. The same Pope consecrated Russia to our Lady in 1952.

The consecration of the world was renewed by Paul VI in 1964 and by John Paul II in 1981.

Shortly before Jacinta died at the age of ten, she said to Lucy, "I have only a short time left before I go to heaven, but you must remain here below to make the world know that our Lord wishes devotion to the Immaculate Heart of Mary established in the world.... Tell everybody that God gives graces through the Immaculate Heart of Mary. Tell them to ask these graces from her, and that the Heart of Jesus wishes to be venerated together with the Immaculate Heart of His Mother. Ask them to plead for peace from the Immaculate Heart of Mary, for the Lord has confided the peace of the world to her."

In obedience to her ecclesiastical superior and her confessor, Lucy revealed a part of the secret confided by our Lady, and it concerns the devotion to the Immaculate Heart of Mary.

Pope Pius XII instituted the Feast of the Immaculate Heart of Mary in 1945, to be celebrated on August 22. Today the Feast is celebrated on the Saturday following the Second Sunday of Pentecost.

THE WORD OF GOD

"The daughter of the King enters all glorious; her raiment is made of spun gold." —Ps 45:14

"She is the brightness of eternal light, the unspotted mirror of the majesty of God, the image of His goodness." —Wis 7:26

"His Mother kept all these things carefully in her Heart." —Lk 2:51

NOVENA PRAYERS

Novena Prayer

IMMACULATE Heart of Mary, full of love for God and mankind, and of compassion for sinners, I consecrate myself entirely to you. I entrust to you the salvation of my soul. May my heart be ever united with yours, so that I may hate sin, love God, and my neighbor, and reach eternal life together with those whom I love.

Mediatrix of All Graces and Mother of Mercy, remember the infinite treasure which your Divine Son has merited by His sufferings and which He has confided to you for us, your children. Filled with confidence in your motherly Heart, which I venerate and love, I come to you with my pressing needs. Through the merits of your loving Heart, and for the sake of the Sacred Heart of Jesus, obtain for me the favor I ask: *(Mention your request).*

Dearest Mother, if what I ask for should not be according to God's Will, pray that I may receive that which will be of greater benefit to my soul. May I experience the kindness of your motherly Heart and the power of your intercession with Jesus during life and at the hour of my death. Amen.

Petitions

IMMACULATE Virgin, conceived without sin, you directed every movement of your most pure Heart toward God and were always obedient to His Divine Will. Obtain for me the grace to hate sin with all my heart and to learn from you to live in perfect resignation to the Will of God.

Mary, I admire that deep humility which troubled your blessed Heart at the message of the Angel Gabriel when he announced that you had been chosen to be the Mother of the Son of the most high God. You considered yourself only God's lowly handmaid. Ashamed at the sight of my own pride, I beg of you the grace of a contrite and humble heart so that I may acknowledge my misery and reach the glory promised to the truly humble of heart.

Blessed Virgin, you kept in your Heart the precious treasure of the words of Jesus your Son and, pondering over the sublime mysteries they contained, you lived only for God. How ashamed I am of my coldness of heart! Dear Mother, obtain for me the grace of meditating always on the holy law of God and of seeking to follow your example in the fervent practice of all the Christian virtues.

Glorious Queen of Martyrs, during the Passion of your Son your holy Heart was cruelly pierced by the sword which had been foretold by the holy and aged Simeon. Obtain for my heart true courage and holy patience to bear the sufferings and trials of this difficult life. May I prove to be your true child by crucifying my flesh and all its desires in the mortification of the Cross.

Mary, Mystical Rose, your amiable Heart, burning with the living fire of love, adopted us as your children at the foot of the Cross, and you thereby became our most tender Mother. Let me feel the sweetness of your motherly Heart and the power of your intercession with Jesus, in all the dangers that I meet with during life, and especially at the dread hour of my death. May my heart be ever united to yours and love Jesus now and forever. Amen.

Prayer

HEAVENLY Father, You prepared the Heart of the Virgin Mary to be a fitting dwelling place for Your Holy Spirit. By her prayers for us may our souls become a more worthy temple of Your glory. Grant this through our Lord Jesus Christ, Your Son, Who lives and reigns with You and the Holy Spirit, one God, forever. Amen.

—AUGUST—

22. THE ASSUMPTION OF MARY

(August 15)

MEDITATION

THE Blessed Virgin Mary obeyed the law of *death,* but her death was rather a peaceful slumber, a gentle separation of the soul from the body. Her soul reached such a degree of love that it seemed unable to rest any longer except in the blissful embrace of the Blessed Trinity. It left her immaculate body and sped to enjoy the blessed vision of God. But soon her beautiful soul was again united to her body which lay peacefully in the tomb, and suddenly Mary stood immortal and glorified, clothed in queenly glory.

As Angels sang their hymns of praise, Mary was *raised on high* to the Kingdom of glory by God's own power. Who can tell the joy of that loving embrace whereby Jesus welcomed and admitted His own Virgin Mother to unending union with Him in the glory of heaven!

Mary's peaceful tomb had been opened by the Apostles and found to be empty. Tradition tells us that beautiful flowers filled the place where her body had once lain, and heavenly music enveloped her empty tomb. The Apostles then realized that she had been taken up into heaven, soul and body.

It was *fitting* that Mary should be assumed into heaven with soul and body. By her Assumption God honored her body that was always the temple in which He dwelt by grace. It was a gate through which the Son of God, the Divine Word, passed to earth and became Man.

It was *fitting* that Mary's holy and virginal body which gave flesh and blood to the God of all sanctity, the Victor over death, should never experience the corruption of the grave. Death and corruption are a result of original sin; but by her Immaculate Conception Mary was preserved from original sin and its effects.

Mary offered herself to suffering and her beloved Son to death for the redemption of mankind; it was *fitting* that she should be united with Him in glory.

We should rejoice that after years of suffering on earth, Mary has at last been taken to the throne prepared for her in heaven where she reigns with her Son. The Church expresses this joy on the solemn feast of the Assumption of the Virgin Mary, August 15, which is also a Holy Day of Obligation.

THE WORD OF GOD

"We know that if the earthly tent in which we live is destroyed we have a building from God, a house in heaven, not made with hands, that will be eternal."

—2 Cor 5:1

"Mary has chosen the best part, and it will not be taken away from her." —Lk 10:42

"A great sign appeared in heaven: a woman clothed with the sun, with the moon under her feet and a crown of twelve stars on her head." —Rev 12:1

NOVENA PRAYERS

Novena Prayer

MARY, Queen Assumed into Heaven, I rejoice that after years of heroic martyrdom on earth, you have at last been taken to the throne prepared for you in heaven by the Holy Trinity.

Lift my heart with you in the glory of your Assumption above the dreadful touch of sin and impurity. Teach me how small earth becomes when viewed from heaven. Make me realize that death is the triumphant gate through which I shall pass to your Son, and that someday my body shall rejoin my soul in the unending bliss of heaven.

From this earth, over which I tread as a pilgrim, I look to you for help. In honor of your Assumption into heaven I ask for this favor: *(Mention your request).*

When my hour of death has come, lead me safely to the presence of Jesus to enjoy the vision of my God for all eternity together with you.

Prayer to the Queen of Heaven and Earth

MARY, Assumed into Heaven, I venerate you as the Queen of heaven and earth. Your own Son led you to a throne of glory in heaven next to His own. As you tasted the bitterness of pain and sorrow with Him on earth, you now enjoy eternal bliss with Him in heaven. I thank Jesus for having put a most beautiful crown upon your head, while all the Angels and Saints acclaim you as their Queen.

Because here below you shared in all the mysteries of our Redemption, Jesus has crowned you not only with glory but with power. He placed you at His right hand that you may dispose of the treasures of grace by a singular title—that of Mother of God.

In the midst of all the Saints you stand as their Queen and ours—dearer to the Heart of God than any creature in God's Kingdom. You pray for your children and distribute to us every grace won by our loving Savior on the Cross.

Queen Assumed into Heaven, may your glorious beauty fill my heart with a distaste for earthly things and an ardent longing for the joys of heaven.

May your merciful eyes glance down upon my struggles and my weakness in this vale of tears. Crown me with the pure robe of innocence and grace here, and with immortality and glory in heaven.

Prayer to Mary Assumed into Heaven

MARY, my dear Mother and mighty Queen, take and receive my poor heart with all its freedom and desires, all its love and all the virtues and graces with which it may be adorned. All I am, all I might be, all I have and hold in the order of nature as well as of grace, I have received from God through your loving intercession, my Lady and Queen. Into your sovereign hands I entrust all, that it may be returned to its noble origin.

Mary, Queen of every heart, accept all that I am and bind me to you with the bonds of love, that I may be yours forever, and may be able to say in all truth: "I belong to Jesus through Mary."

My Mother, assumed into heaven, I love you. Give me a greater love for Jesus and for you.

Mary, Assumed into Heaven and Queen of the Universe, ever-Virgin Mother of God, obtain peace and salvation for us through your prayers, for you have given birth to Christ the Lord, the Savior of all mankind.

Prayer

ALMIGHTY, ever-living God, You raised to eternal glory the body and soul of the immaculate Virgin Mary, Mother of Your Son. Grant that our minds may always be directed heavenward and that we may deserve to share in her glory.

—SEPTEMBER—

23. THE MOTHER OF SORROWS

(September 15)

MEDITATION

THE seven Sorrows of the Blessed Virgin Mary that have made the strongest appeal to devotion are: the prophecy of Simeon, the flight into Egypt, the three days' loss of Jesus, the meeting with Jesus carrying His Cross, His Death on Calvary, His being taken down from the Cross, and His burial in the tomb.

Simeon foretold to the Mother the opposition the Redeemer would arouse. When she offered her forty-day-old Child to God in the Temple, he said, "This Child is destined for the fall and for the rise of many in Israel, and for a sign that shall be contradicted. And your own soul a sword shall pierce" (Lk 2:34-35).

Mary's sorrow on Calvary was deeper than any sorrow ever felt on earth, for no mother in all the world had a heart as tender as the Heart of the Mother of God. As there was no love like her love, there was no sorrow like her sorrow. She bore her sufferings for us that we might enjoy the graces of Redemption. She suffered willingly in order to prove her love for us, for true love is proved by sacrifice.

It was not because she was the Mother of God that Mary could bear her sorrows, but because she saw things from His point of view and not from her own—or rather, she had made His point of view hers. We should do the same. The Mother of Sorrows will be on hand to help us.

Devotion to the Sorrows of Mary is the source of great graces because it leads into the depths of the Heart of Christ. If we think frequently of the false pleasures of this world, we shall embrace patiently the sorrows and sufferings of this life, and we shall be penetrated with a sorrow for sin.

The Church urges us to give ourselves over to the love of Mary completely and bear our cross patiently with the Mother of Sorrows. She earnestly wants to help us to bear our daily crosses because it was on Calvary that her dying Son entrusted us to her care. It was His last Will that she should be our Mother. It was also His last Will that we love His Mother as He did.

THE WORD OF GOD

"This Child is destined for the fall and for the rise of many in Israel, and for a sign that shall be contradicted. And your own soul a sword shall pierce, that the thoughts of many hearts may be revealed." —Lk 2:34-35

"His Mother said to [Jesus]: 'Son, why have You done this to us? Behold, Your father and I have been anxiously searching for You.' " —Lk 2:48

"All you who pass by the way, look and see whether there is any sorrow like my sorrow." —Lam 1:12

NOVENA PRAYERS

Novena Prayer

MOST holy and afflicted Virgin, Mother of Sorrows and Queen of Martyrs! You stood motionless at the foot of the Cross beneath your dying Son. Through the sword of grief which pierced you then, through the unceasing suffering of your life of sorrow, and the bliss which now fully repays you for your past trials and afflictions, look upon me with a mother's tenderness and have pity on me, as I pray before you to venerate your sorrows, and place my request with childlike confidence in the sanctuary of your wounded Heart.

I beg of you to present to Jesus Christ, in union with the infinite merits of His Passion and Death, your sufferings at the foot of the Cross, and through the power of both, to grant my request: *(Mention your request).*

To whom shall I turn in my needs and miseries, if not to you, Mother of mercy? You drank so deeply of the chalice of your Son that you can sympathize with the sufferings of those who are still in this valley of tears.

Offer to our Divine Savior the sufferings He bore on the Cross that the memory of them may draw His mercy upon me, a sinner. Refuge of sinners and hope of all mankind, accept my petition and grant it, if it be according to the Will of God.

Lord Jesus Christ, I offer You the merits of Mary, Your Mother and ours, as she stood beneath the Cross, in order that by her loving intercession I may obtain the happy fruits of Your Passion and Death.

Offering

MARY, most holy Virgin and Queen of Martyrs, accept the sincere homage of my childlike love. Into your heart, pierced by so many swords, welcome my poor soul. Receive it as the companion of your sorrows at the foot of the Cross, on which Jesus died for the redemption of the world.

With you, sorrowful Virgin, I will gladly suffer all the trials, sufferings, and afflictions which it shall please our Lord to send me. I offer them all to you in memory of your sorrows so that every thought of my mind and every beat of my heart may be an act of compassion and of love for you.

Dearest Mother, have pity on me, reconcile me to your Divine Son Jesus, keep me in His grace, and assist me in my last agony, so that I may meet you in heaven together with your loving Son.

Hymn—Stabat Mater

AT the Cross her station keeping,
Stood the mournful Mother weeping,
Close to Jesus to the last.
Through her heart, His sorrow sharing,
All His bitter anguish bearing,
Lo, the piercing sword has passed!

O, how sad and sore distressed,
Was that Mother highly blessed
Of the sole-begotten One.
Christ above in torment hangs,
She beneath beholds the pangs
Of her dying glorious Son.

Is there one who would not weep
'Whelmed in miseries so deep
Christ's dear Mother to behold?
Can the human heart refrain
From partaking in the pain,
In that Mother's pain untold?

Bruised, derided, cursed, defiled,
She beheld her tender Child,
All with bloody scourges rent.
For the sins of His own nation
Saw Him hang in desolation
Till His Spirit forth He sent.

O sweet Mother! fount of love,
Touch my spirit from above,
Make my heart with yours accord.
Make me feel as you have felt.
Make my soul to glow and melt
With the love of Christ, my Lord.

Holy Mother, pierce me through.
In my heart each wound renew
Of my Savior crucified.
Let me share with you His pain,
Who for all our sins was slain,
Who for me in torments died.

Let me mingle tears with you,
Mourning Him who mourned for me,
All the days that I may live.
By the Cross with you to stay,
There with you to weep and pray,
Is all I ask of you to give.

Virgin of all virgins blest!
Listen to my fond request:
Let me share your grief Divine.
Let me, to my latest breath,
In my body bear the death
Of your dying Son Divine.

Wounded with his every wound,
Steep my soul till it has swooned
In His very Blood away.
Be to me, O Virgin, nigh,
Lest in flames I burn and die,
In His awe-full judgment day.

Christ, when You shall call me hence,
Be Your Mother my defense,
Be Your Cross my victory.
While my body here decays,
May my soul Your goodness praise,
Safe in heaven eternally.
Amen. Alleluia.

Prayer

FATHER, it was Your Will that the compassionate Mother of Your Son should stand near the Cross on which He was glorified. Grant that Your Church, having shared in Christ's Passion, may also participate in His Resurrection. We ask this through our Lord, Jesus Christ, Your Son, Who lives and reigns with You and the Holy Spirit, one God, forever. Amen.

—OCTOBER—

24. ROSARY NOVENA

(Our Lady of the Holy Rosary, October 7)

MEDITATION

THE Rosary is a favorite means of devotion to the Blessed Virgin Mary, recommended by the Popes over many centuries. It consists of various elements:

a) *Contemplation,* in union with Mary, of a series of mysteries of salvation, distributed into three cycles. These mysteries express the joy of the Messianic times, the suffering of Christ, and the glory of the Risen Lord which fills the Church. This contemplation by its very nature encourages practical reflection and provides norms for living.

b) *The Lord's Prayer,* which by reason of its immense value is at the basis of Christian prayer and ennobles that prayer in its various expressions.

c) The litany-like succession of the *Hail Mary,* which is made up of the Angel's greeting to the Virgin (Lk 1:28) and of Elizabeth's greeting (Lk 1:42), followed by the Church's own prayer. The continued series of Hail Marys is the special characteristic of the Rosary, and their number (150) is divided into decades attached to the individual mysteries.

d) The doxology *Glory be to the Father* concludes the prayer with the glorifying of God Who is One and Three, from Whom, through Whom, and in Whom all things have their being (Rom 11:36).

In her sixth and last apparition at Fatima, October 13, 1917, the Blessed Virgin insisted on the recitation of the Rosary as a powerful means for the conversion of Russia and for peace in the world. When Lucy asked, "Who are you and what do you want?" Our Lady replied: "I am the Lady of the Rosary, and I have come to warn the faithful to amend their lives and ask pardon for their sins. They must not continue to offend our Lord who is already so deeply offended. They must say the Rosary."

Through the prayer of the Rosary untold blessings have been showered down upon all humankind throughout the ages. Through the Rosary today as in past times of peril that have threatened civilization, Mary has again come to save all humankind from the evils that overwhelm us.

But the Rosary is especially most helpful in bringing back home life to its full splendor, by raising the family to a higher family circle where God is Father and Mary is Mother and we are all children of God. The Family Rosary is a practical way to strengthen the unity of family life.

THE WORD OF GOD

"Who is she that comes forth like the morning rising, as beautiful as the moon, as bright as the sun, as awe-inspiring as an army in battle array?" —Song 6:10

"You are as beautiful as Tirzah [early capital of Northern Israel], as comely as Jerusalem, as awe-inspiring as an army in battle array." —Song 6:4

"Listen to me, my faithful children: blossom like roses planted near a stream of water; send out your fragrance like incense, and break forth in blossoms like the lily. Scatter your fragrance and sing a hymn of praise; bless the Lord for all His works." —Sir 39:13-14

NOVENA PRAYERS

Novena Prayer

MY dearest Mother Mary, behold me, your child, in prayer at your feet. Accept this Holy Rosary, which I offer you in accordance with your requests at Fatima, as a proof of my tender love for you, for the intentions of the Sacred Heart of Jesus, in atonement for the offenses committed against your Immaculate Heart, and for this special favor which I earnestly request in my Rosary Novena: *(Mention your request).*

I beg you to present my petition to your Divine Son. If you will pray for me, I cannot be refused. I know, dearest Mother, that you want me to seek God's holy Will concerning my request. If what I ask for should not be granted, pray that I may receive that which will be of greater benefit to my soul.

I offer you this spiritual "Bouquet of Roses" because I love you. I put all my confidence in you, since your prayers before God are most powerful. For the greater glory of God and for the sake of Jesus, your loving Son, hear and grant my prayer. Sweet Heart of Mary, be my salvation.

THE HOLY ROSARY

ON the Cross: In the Name of the Father, etc. I believe in God, the Father Almighty, Creator of heaven and earth; and in Jesus Christ, His only Son, our Lord; Who was conceived by the Holy Spirit, born of the Virgin Mary, suffered under Pontius Pilate, was crucified, died, and was buried. He descended into hell; the third day he arose again from the dead; he ascended into heaven, and sits at the right hand of God, the Father Almighty; from thence he shall come to judge the living and the dead. I believe in the Holy Spirit, the Holy Catholic Church, the Communion of Saints, the forgiveness of sins, the resurrection of the body, and life everlasting. Amen.

On the first large bead: Our Father, etc.

On the next three beads: For an increase of faith, hope, and charity. Hail Mary, etc. (*3 times*).

Glory be to the Father, etc.

Fatima prayer (after each decade): "O my Jesus, forgive us our sins, save us from the fire of hell, take all souls to heaven, and help especially those most in need of Your mercy."

FIRST, FOURTH, SEVENTH DAY

1st Joyful Mystery

The Annunciation

Our Father . . .

JESUS, at the Annunciation God proposes the mystery of Your Incarnation which will be fulfilled in the Blessed Virgin when she shall have given her free consent. Through the Angel Gabriel You invite her to become Your Mother. It seems as though You await the response of the humanity to which You wish to unite Yourself.

Full of faith, Mary gives her reply: "I am the servant of the Lord. Let it be done to me as you say." At this moment You, the Divine Word, the Second Person of the Holy Trinity, take flesh of the Virgin Mary and become Man, for the Angel said to her, "The Holy Spirit will come upon you and the power of the Most High will overshadow you; hence, the holy offspring to be born will be called Son of God."

This is the greatest event in the history of the world, for the salvation of human beings depends upon it. I thank You for having loved me so much as to become Man to save my soul. I thank you for having chosen the Virgin Mary as Your Mother. This mystery has earned for her the most glorious of her titles, that of Mother of God, which makes her all-powerful with You, her Divine Son. Through Your Mother's intercession grant me the grace to save my soul.
Hail Mary. *(Ten times)*
Glory be to the Father . . .

"O my Jesus, forgive us our sins, save us from the fire of hell, take all souls to heaven, and help especially those most in need of Your mercy."

2nd Joyful Mystery
The Visitation

JESUS, in God's design the Visitation is the occasion when You reveal the fact of Your Incarnation and Your Mother's role as the dispenser of all graces. You work Your first miracle in Mary's womb by stirring the unborn John and making Elizabeth conscious of Your presence. You brought grace upon the earth and Your love made You bestow it at once through Your loving Mother. John the Baptist receives its first gift because his task is so closely connected with Your Person.

In this mystery You wish to show us that Your Mother is the instrument and means by which You impart to us Your graces. I believe that all graces have their source in You, the Head of the Mystical Body, the Church. But these graces reach us, the members, through Mary, as if she were the neck of that Body. Where Mary is, there the springs of heavenly blessings flow more freely and more richly, because she bears in herself You, the Source of all grace. It is Your Will that she impart this grace to others. I thank You for making Your Mother the Mediatrix of All Graces.

3rd Joyful Mystery

The Birth of Our Lord

JESUS, with Mary and Joseph I kneel down in devout worship as I gaze upon You lying in Your crib. You wish to enter the world as a Child in order to prove Yourself to be true Man, for Your weeping and Your need for rest and nourishment are just so many proofs of Your true human nature. You become Human that we may be able to see You, listen to You, imitate You, and unite ourselves to You. Even though You are God, You are now able to suffer for us, atone for our sins, and merit graces for our souls. It is through the flesh that human beings turn away from God; it is in taking on the flesh that God delivers them.

But You become Man also that we may become like God. In exchange for the Humanity which You take from us, you wish to make us share in Your Divinity by sanctifying grace, that You may take complete possession of us.

May the mystery of Your birth bring me the grace to be born again spiritually and live a new Divine life, more free from sin and from all attachment to myself and creatures—a life for God alone. As it was Mary's joy to form You in her own body, may her joy now be to form You in my soul.

4th Joyful Mystery

The Presentation in the Temple

JESUS, by the union of Your Human Nature with the second Person of the Blessed Trinity You were consecrated to God. But this ceremony of presentation is Your first external consecration to Your priestly mission. As the Anointed of the Lord, the Long-Desired of Nations, You are brought for the first time into Your Temple, into Your Father's house.

In Your Mother's arms You offer Yourself to Your heavenly Father to be the Victim of our Redemption, as in future years You will continue to offer Yourself daily at Mass in the hands of numberless priests. No one can hear the words You utter while offering Yourself, but the secret thoughts of Your Sacred Heart are expressed by the lips of Your Blessed Mother as she offers You for the salvation of the world.

The aged Simeon, enlightened by the Holy Spirit, recognizes You as the Messiah. Joyfully he takes You in his arms and proclaims You to be "a revealing Light to the Gentiles."

You humbly and fervently offer Yourself to the Father by the hands of the ancient priesthood. Never has a greater offering been made to God in this Temple. The Most Holy Trinity and all heaven look down on it with delight.

5th Joyful Mystery

The Finding in the Temple

JESUS, I see You as a Boy of twelve in the Temple, sitting in the midst of teachers who are amazed at Your wisdom and charmed by Your personality. It is here that Mary and Joseph find You after having sought You with sorrow for three days.

This mystery reveals to me Your devoted love and tender reverence for Your Father. God alone is in Your heart, and nothing but His Will rules there; every other claim has to be silent before it.

You appear in the Temple to show that You must be about Your Father's work. Although you have a Mother and owe her loving obedience, You also have a Father Who is greater, and whose Will and command must be given first place. That Will and command is the promotion of His honor and the salvation of souls, which is Your life-work.

Let the glory of God and the salvation of souls, especially my own, be my only real concern in life. I wish to be attached to God alone by love as You always were, and to do His Holy Will in all things. May I put out of my heart desires for worldly things, and give God the first right to all that I have, especially to my love.

SECOND, FIFTH, EIGHTH DAY
1st Sorrowful Mystery
The Agony in the Garden

JESUS, the time has come for Your holy Passion to begin. You already feel the burden of suffering weigh heavily upon You in the Garden of Olives.

Yours is the suffering of the soul. Fear takes hold of You—fear caused by the certainty and nearness of Your Death and the sufferings that are to bring it about. You experience disgust at the thought of the sins for which You are to suffer so much. How terrible are these sins of all races and ages in all their vileness and malice as compared with God's supreme authority, infinite goodness, justice, and beauty!

Sadness fills the very depths of Your soul, sadness caused by the knowledge of the small result You will gain by all Your sacrifices, how people will neglect Your Church, or misuse it to their own ruin. All these dreadful pictures rise before You and cut You to the very Heart. You are sorrowful unto death.

You pray: "Father, if it is Your will, take this cup from Me; yet not My will but Yours be done." Your sweat becomes like drops of blood falling to the ground.

Help me to show my gratitude for Your generosity by true contrition for my sins and by a sincere love for You, my best Friend and my God.

2nd Sorrowful Mystery

The Scourging

JESUS, Pilate sentences You to be beaten into a pitiable condition in order to arouse the compassion of the Jews. You are to endure the dreadful suffering of a Roman scourging, cruel enough to be reserved only for murderers and slaves—and You are the Son of God!

Your virginal flesh is unveiled in the sight of harsh and inhuman soldiers. After Your wrists have been bound with cords and Your Body drawn up so that Your face is turned to the pillar, they begin their blood work. The strokes of the scourges fall with terrible force upon Your bare back and shoulders. Your body trembles with pain beneath the mighty blows, unlimited in number and severity, that burn like fire upon Your skin and cause it to break and swell.

Your Precious Blood oozes forth and trickles down in little streams to the dirty floor. Pain pierces its way to Your very soul, and forces tears from Your eyes and moans from Your lips.

Love makes You endure the scourge of suffering to prevent the scourge of God's just wrath from falling upon me to atone for my sins of impurity. I thank You for this love, and I beg You to help me love You in return and turn away from every sin.

3rd Sorrowful Mystery

The Crowning with Thorns

JESUS, the soldiers make You a mock-king. They tear the clothes from Your bleeding shoulders and cover You with a soldier's cast-off cloak to serve as Your royal robe. They make You sit down upon the broken base of a pillar as upon a throne. Above Your tearful eyes they set a crown of sharp thorns and brutally force it down into Your scalp and entangle it in Your hair. This crown of shame is man's highest contempt for Your Divine Kingship.

As a scepter they put into Your right hand a reed. You sit there, bowed with pain, the picture of complete wretchedness, and yet You are the living God Who at this moment wield a scepter of might over innumerable Angel-hosts. You are the Messiah, the Long-Expected of the nations, and yet you are mocked as a fool. You are the Creator of the universe and all the living, and yet Your creatures give You a crown of shame.

I now bend my knee before You, and pledge unending loyalty to You, my Divine King. Once I bent the knee in contempt of You and Your holy commandments; now I bend it in sincerest love and adoration.

4th Sorrowful Mystery

The Carrying of the Cross

JESUS, You and the Cross are at last together, and Your Heart is already nailed to it. How tenderly You fix Your gaze upon it, press it to Your Heart, and lovingly kiss it. Although You receive the Cross from the kindly hand of Your Father in heaven, it is really I who place its heavy load upon Your bruised shoulder.

The Cross is the symbol of Your tenderest love, the altar on which You are to be sacrificed as the Lamb of God Who takes away the sins of the world. The Cross is the instrument of Your mercy, the trophy of Your victory, and yet You must now feel the disgrace of it as You begin Your last journey for love of me.

I can never understand the depth of suffering to which You consent in receiving Your Cross. Your whole being is crushed by the weight of my sins. You have taught me that Your command to follow You to Calvary is a condition of everlasting happiness. Teach me to bear my pains and disappointments patiently in atonement for my sins. Make my cross of life Your own, and help me to love my sufferings as You love Your Cross.

5th Sorrowful Mystery

The Crucifixion

JESUS, at last Calvary is reached. The soldiers seize You roughly and strip the garments from Your torn body. I see how the wounds inflicted by the scourges are again torn open when You are stripped of Your garments. Strip me of all sinfulness and clothe my poor soul with Your own purity and holiness.

Into each of Your hands and then into Your feet the executioners hammer a heavy nail. Now You lie fastened upon Your hard bed, Your deathbed, with Your head resting upon the painful pillow of Your crown of thorns. Your glances are directed upward to Your Father in entire resignation to

His Divine Will, as you pray, "Father forgive them, for they do not know what they are doing." Pray to the Father to forgive me, for my sins nailed You to the Cross, but I, too, did not know what I was doing.

Strong arms lift You aloft and You are left hanging there between heaven and earth, like a criminal, to die slowly amid the terrible torture of body and bitter sadness of soul.

Your fading eyes gaze into the darkened heavens as You cry out with a loud voice, "Father, into Your hands I commend My spirit." Then You bend Your thorn-crowned head in submission to the Will of Your Father and to death. You have died that I might live.

I thank You for Your love for me. May I always live for love of You.

THIRD, SIXTH, NINTH DAY

1st Glorious Mystery

The Resurrection

JESUS, after Your burial Your enemies sealed the opening of Your tomb and set the guards; they went their way rejoicing that they had conquered You at last. But, by Your own Divine power You rise, as You promised, a glorious Victor.

The earth quakes as You come forth from the tomb, and the guards tremble with fear. Your body now shines like the sun. The wounds of Your hands and feet sparkle like precious jewels. Death is conquered, its victory broken, its sting destroyed. You triumph not for Yourself alone, but that I too may triumph over the grave.

May this mystery strengthen my hope in another and a better life after death, the resurrection of my body on the last day, and an eternity of happiness. I firmly hope that You will keep Your promise to me and raise me up glorified. Through Your glorious Resurrection I hope that You will make my body like Your own in glory and life, and permit me to dwell with You in heaven.

2nd Glorious Mystery
The Ascension

JESUS, on the fortieth day after Your Resurrection, after having trained Your Apostles for their high calling to establish the Kingdom of God on earth, You go with them to the Mount of Olives. Standing on the summit of that same mountain which had been the scene of the beginning of Your Passion, and streaming with light as at the moment of Your Transfiguration,

You prepare to ascend on high to where the glories of heaven await You.

You bless Your loving Mother and Your Apostles and disciples and bid them farewell. A cloud receives You out of their sight. How deep is their sorrow at parting from You! How keen their longing to follow You!

The countless blessed spirits whom You have released from limbo accompany You as the first fruits of the Redemption. All the hosts of heaven's Angels come out to meet You, the Savior of the world. As You take Your place beside Your heavenly Father, the whole court of heaven gives forth a glorious song of praise. I rejoice with You in this perfect attainment of Your glory. When the struggle of this life is over, give me the grace to share Your joy and triumph in heaven for all eternity.

3rd Glorious Mystery

The Descent of the Holy Spirit

JESUS, I thank You for fulfilling Your gracious promise: "I will ask the Father and He will give You another Paraclete, to be with You always."

Holy Spirit, on the fiftieth day after the Resurrection of Jesus, in the midst of a mighty wind, You descend upon the Blessed Virgin, the Apostles and disciples in the Upper Room.

You appear under the form of tongues of fire, because you fill the Apostles with truth and prepare them to bear witness to Jesus. You pour forth in them Your love ardent as a flame, powerful as a violent wind, for You are the personal Love of the Father and the Son in the life of God.

Being filled with Your Divine grace, they go forth fearlessly to preach Jesus Christ with great power and success. You come upon the Infant Church to give it Divine life, to enlighten and preserve it from error and to make it perfect in holiness.

You are, in the Church, what the soul is to the body: the spirit that animates it and protects its unity. Your Divine action produces marvels of grace in the souls of people. Glorify Jesus by spreading His Church throughout the world.

May Your gift of grace enable me one day to gaze upon the sight of God in all His beauty, and to enjoy without end the sweetness and bliss of Your Divine love!

4th Glorious Mystery

The Assumption of Mary

MARY, you obey the law of death, but your death is rather a peaceful slumber, a gentle separation of the soul from the body. Your soul reaches such a degree of love that it seems unable to rest any longer except in the blissful love of the Blessed Trinity.

Your soul sweetly speeds to enjoy the blessed vision of God, and leaves your immaculate body silent and motionless, though very beautiful, in the sleep of death. But soon your fair soul is again united to your body which lies peacefully in the tomb, and suddenly you stand immortal and glorified, clothed in queenly glory. As the Angels sing their hymns of praise, you are raised on high to the Kingdom of glory by God's own power.

There the heavenly citizens bow their heads in humble reverence before you. Who can tell the sweetness of that loving embrace whereby Jesus welcomes and admits you, his own Virgin Mother, to unending union with Him in the glory of heaven.

Your peaceful tomb has been reopened by the Apostles and found to be empty. Beautiful flowers fill the place where your body has lain, and heavenly music is heard about your empty tomb. The Apostles now realize that you have been taken up into heaven, soul and body.

Help me in my life's true work: to choose virtue and reject sin. Protect me from the danger of temptation, and lead me in the path of virtue till the day of my judgment, that I may share your glory forever.

5th Glorious Mystery

Crowning of Mary in Heaven

MARY, in spirit I behold how Jesus leads you to a throne of glory in heaven next to His own. As you tasted the bitterness of pain and sorrow with Him on earth, you will now enjoy the sweetness of eternal bliss with Him in heaven. You have worn a crown of thorns with Jesus; you will now wear a crown of gold and precious stones even as He does.

I rejoice with you as I see Him put this most beautiful crown upon your head, while all the Angels and Saints acclaim you as their Queen. Your immaculate Heart beats in unison with the Divine Heart of Jesus, which is now shedding upon you with great delight the love of God made Man. You bow to the Most Blessed Trinity in deepest humility and again utter your prayer of praise: "My being proclaims the greatness of the Lord, my spirit finds joy in God my savior, for God Who is mighty has done great things for me, holy is His Name." You then turn with joy to the Angels and Saints and graciously accept their homage.

May the glorious beauty of your crowning in heaven fill my heart with an ardent longing for the joys of heaven. Through your intercession and tender mercy may I reach the glorious Kingdom of Heaven, there to be happy with Jesus and you for all eternity!

Prayer

℣. Pray for us, O holy Mother of God.

℟. *That we may be made worthy of the promises of Christ.*

LET us pray. God, Whose only-begotten Son by His Life, Death, and Resurrection obtained for us the rewards of eternal salvation grant, we beg of You, that meditating upon these mysteries in the most Holy Rosary of the Blessed Virgin Mary, we may both imitate what they contain and obtain what they promise. Through Christ our Lord. ℟. *Amen.*

—DECEMBER—

25. THE IMMACULATE CONCEPTION

(December 8)

MEDITATION

THE Church teaches that from the first moment of her conception the Blessed Virgin Mary possessed sanctifying grace, even the fullness of grace, with the infused virtues and gifts of the Holy Spirit. Yet she remained subject to death and other pains and miseries of life that her Son Himself willed to undergo.

Mary was "in the first instant of her conception, by the singular grace and privilege of the all-powerful God, in virtue of the merits of Jesus Christ, Savior of the human race, preserved from all stain of original sin."

This article of faith is founded upon Scripture and upon the constant Tradition of the Church. Since God Himself had announced from the beginning of the world that Mary was destined "to crush the head" of the infernal serpent through her Divine Son, she could not have begun her life by being wounded herself by his poisonous bite and subject to his power. The Archangel Gabriel called her "full of grace" because she never was deprived of sanctifying grace, and consequently she possessed this grace in the first moment of her conception.

The Fathers and writers of the Church compare Mary to the ark of Noah which alone escaped the universal deluge; to the thornbush which Moses saw burning, but not consumed; to the enclosed garden; to the rod of Aaron which, when laid in the ark, budded and blossomed without having taken root; to the fleece of Gideon which remained dry while the ground all around it became moist with dew. They look upon Mary as the Queen who came from the Most High, perfect, beautiful, and without original sin; as the paradise of innocence which God Himself planted and protected against all the attacks of the poisonous serpent.

Reason, too, approves of Mary's Immaculate Conception, for this privilege corresponds with her sublime vocation. She was the throne of God, the wonderful palace in which the Son of God chose to dwell for nine months. Her womb was the chosen place honored by the mysterious working of the Holy Spirit. If everything that comes in contact with God must be pure and immaculate, purity was necessary for her, the vessel in which the Son of God formed His Flesh and Blood. Her Immaculate Conception is a brilliant witness to the sanctity of Jesus, her Son.

If Jesus, the Son of God, could choose for His Mother her who pleased Him most, He would surely choose one acceptable to the Blessed Trinity and worthy of the great honor for which she was destined. Mary was, therefore not only free from all actual sin, but she also remained exempt from original sin; otherwise, she would not have been a Mother suitable for Jesus Christ, the Son of God.

As Eve received natural life from Adam, Mary received spiritual life, the life of grace, through her Son. If Eve was originally immaculate, Mary, who is superior to Eve in merits, could not be inferior to her in dignity. Since Eve was immaculate in her formation, Mary must have been immaculate in her conception.

God Himself has testified to Mary's Immaculate Conception by miracles. Who can number the wonders that have been wrought at Lourdes, where she appeared eighteen times and declared to Bernadette and to the world: "I am the Immaculate Conception," just four years after this doctrine was defined as a dogma of faith? Mary declared to the whole world her approval of this doctrine and that she was not only immaculately conceived, but that she is the Immaculate Conception.

We should be grateful to God for the grace of Baptism by which we were cleansed from original sin and spiritually regenerated and sanctified. We ought to ask the Immaculate Virgin Mary to guard us against every sin, above all against every mortal sin, lest we lose the grace of God, infinitely greater than all the riches of the world.

The solemn feast of the Immaculate Conception, a Holy Day of Obligation, is celebrated on December 8. The Immaculate Conception is honored also on the feast of Our Lady of Lourdes, February 11, and in the devotion of the Miraculous Medal.

THE WORD OF GOD

"You are the glory of Jerusalem, you are the joy of Israel, you are the honor of our people. . . . May you be blessed by the Lord Almighty forever and ever."

—Jud 15:9-10

"I will greatly rejoice in the Lord, and my soul shall be joyful in my God. For He has clothed me with a robe of salvation, and He has covered me with a mantle of justice, . . . like a bride adorned with her jewels." —Isa 61:10

"A great sign appeared in heaven: a woman clothed with the sun, with the moon under her feet, and on her head a crown of twelve stars." —Rev 12:1

NOVENA PRAYERS

Novena Prayer

IMMACULATE Virgin Mary, you were pleasing in the sight of God from the first moment of your conception in the womb of your mother, St. Anne. You were chosen to be the Mother of Jesus Christ, the Son of God. I believe the teaching of Holy Mother the Church, that in the first instant of your conception, by the singular grace and privilege of Almighty God, in virtue of the merits of Jesus Christ, Savior of the human race and your beloved Son, you were preserved from all stain of original sin. I thank God for this wonderful privilege and grace He bestowed upon you as I honor your Immaculate Conception.

Look graciously upon me as I implore this special favor: *(Mention your request).*

Virgin Immaculate, Mother of God and my Mother, from your throne in heaven turn your eyes of pity upon me. Filled with confidence in your goodness and power, I beg you to help me in this journey of life, which is so full of dangers for my soul. I entrust myself entirely to you, that I may never be the slave of the devil through sin, but may always live a humble and pure life. I consecrate myself to you forever, for my only desire is to love your Divine Son Jesus.

Mary, since none of your devout servants has ever perished, may I, too, be saved. Amen.

A Prayer of Saint Ephrem

BLESSED Virgin, immaculate and pure, you are the sinless Mother of your Son, Who is the mighty Lord of the universe. Since you are holy and inviolate, the hope of the hopeless and sinful, I sing your praises. I praise you as full of every grace, for you bore the God-Man. I venerate you; I invoke you and implore your aid.

Holy and Immaculate Virgin, help me in every need that presses upon me and free me from all the temptations of the devil. Be my intercessor and advocate at the hour of death and judgment. Deliver me from the fire that is not extinguished and from the outer darkness. Make me worthy of the glory of your Son, O dearest and most kind Virgin Mother. You indeed are my most secure and only hope for you are holy in the sight of God, to whom be honor and glory, majesty and power forever. Amen.

Prayer to Mary Immaculate

MARY, Mother of God, your greatness began at the first instant of your existence with the privilege of your Immaculate Conception. After Almighty God and the Sacred Humanity of Jesus, there is no being so great as you. It is true, you are a creature, and, therefore, far beneath the Supreme Being. But you are a creature so holy and so perfect that you are superior to all other creatures. God alone could make you so holy and so beautiful, and He did so to make you worthy of the dignity of being the Mother of Jesus, the Son of God, the Divine Word.

It was fitting that you, a Virgin Mother, should conceive the Man who was also the Son of God. It was fitting that you should be adorned with the greatest purity ever possible to a creature. You are the Virgin to whom God the Father decreed to give His only Son—the Divine Word, equal to Himself in all things—that entering the natural order He might become your Son as well as His. You are the immaculate Virgin whom the Son Himself chose to make His Mother. You are the immaculate Virgin whom the Holy Spirit willed to make His bride and in whom He would work the tremendous miracle of the Incarnation. The privilege of the Immaculate Conception was suitable to your dignity.

Mary, my immaculate Mother, help me to imitate your sinlessness by keeping my soul free from every willful sin by the faithful observance of God's commandments. Help me to imitate your fullness of grace by receiving Holy Communion frequently, where I shall obtain the sanctifying grace that will make my soul holy and pleasing to God, and the actual graces I need to practice virtue. Through prayer may grace fill my soul with the life of God and transform me into a living image of Jesus, just as you were.

Prayer

FATHER, You prepared the Virgin Mary to be the worthy Mother of Your Son. You made it possible for her to share beforehand in the salvation Your Son, Jesus Christ, would bring by His death, and kept her without sin from the first moment of her conception. Give us the grace by her prayers ever to live in Your presence without sin. We ask this through the same Christ our Lord. Amen.

26. THE MIRACULOUS MEDAL

(December 8)

MEDITATION

THE medal of the Immaculate Conception, commonly called the Miraculous Medal, was manifested to a spiritual daughter of Saint Vincent de Paul, Saint Catherine Labouré. This took place in the chapel of the Motherhouse of the Sisters of Charity, 140 rue du Bac, Paris, France.

Sister Catherine, during her novitiate days, received extraordinary favors from God, such as visions of the heart of Saint Vincent and manifestations of our Lord in the Blessed Sacrament. In 1830 she was blessed with the apparitions of Mary Immaculate to which we owe the Miraculous Medal.

Saint Catherine describes the apparition of our Lady on November 27, 1830, in these words: "Her feet rested on a white globe. I saw rings on her fingers, and each ring was set with gems. The larger gems emitted greater rays and the smaller gems, smaller rays. I could not express what I saw, the beauty and the brilliance of the dazzling rays. A voice said, 'They are the symbols of the graces I shed upon those who ask for them.'

"A frame formed round the Blessed Virgin. Within it was written in letters of gold: 'O Mary, conceived without sin, pray for us who have recourse to you.' Then the voice said, 'Have a Medal struck after this model. All who wear it will receive great graces; they should wear it around the neck.' At this instant the tableau seemed to turn, and I beheld the reverse of the Medal: a large 'M' surmounted by a bar and a cross; beneath the 'M' were the Hearts of Jesus and Mary, the one crowned with thorns, the other pierced with a sword."

When Saint Catherine related the vision to her confessor, he asked her whether she had seen any writing on the back of the Medal. She answered that she had seen none at all. He told her to ask the Blessed Virgin what to put there. The Sister prayed to Mary a long time and one day during meditation she seemed to hear a voice saying, "The 'M' and the two hearts express enough."

The Medal was made according to our Lady's design. It was freely circulated and in a short time was worn by millions. Many graces were given and blessings bestowed until the little Medal of the Immaculate Conception became known by the name it bears today, the Miraculous Medal.

THE WORD OF GOD

"All the words of my mouth are sincere. . . . They are all clear to the person of intelligence and right to those

who arrive at knowledge. Take my instruction in preference to silver, and knowledge rather than fine gold."
—Prov 8:8-10

"I love those who love me, and those who diligently look for me find me. Riches and honor are with me, dazzling wealth and prosperity. My fruit is better than gold, even the finest of gold, and my products are better than choice silver."
—Prov 8:17-19

"Children, listen to me: Happy are those who keep my ways. Heed instruction and be wise, and do not refuse it."
—Prov 8:32-33

NOVENA PRAYERS

Opening Prayer

COME, Holy Spirit, fill the hearts of Your faithful, and kindle in them the fire of Your love. Send forth Your Spirit, and they shall be created; and You shall renew the face of the earth.

O God, You instructed the hearts of the faithful by the light of the Holy Spirit. Grant us in the same Spirit to be truly wise and ever to rejoice in His consolation, through Jesus Christ our Lord. Amen.

O Mary, conceived without sin, pray for us who have recourse to you. *(3 times.)*

Lord Jesus Christ, You have been pleased to glorify by numberless miracles the Blessed Virgin Mary, immaculate from the first moment of her conception. Grant that all who devoutly implore her protection on earth may eternally enjoy Your presence in heaven, Who, with the Father and the Holy Spirit, live and reign, God, forever and ever. Amen.

Lord Jesus Christ, for the accomplishment of Your works, You have chosen the weak things of the world, that no flesh may glory in Your sight. And for a better and more widely diffused belief in the Immaculate Conception of Your Mother, You have wished that the Miraculous Medal be manifested to Saint Catherine Labouré. Grant, we beseech You, that filled with like humility, we may glorify this mystery by word and work. Amen.

Memorare

REMEMBER, O most gracious Virgin Mary, that never was it known that anyone who fled to your protection, implored your help, or sought your intercession, was left unaided. Inspired with this confidence, I fly to you, O Virgin of virgins, my Mother. To you I come, before you I stand, sinful and sorrowful. O Mother of the Word Incarnate, despise not my petitions, but in your mercy hear and answer me. Amen.

NOVENA PRAYER

IMMACULATE Virgin Mary, Mother of our Lord Jesus Christ and our Mother, penetrated with the most lively confidence in your all-powerful and never-failing intercession, manifested so often through the Miraculous Medal, we your loving and trustful children implore you to obtain for us the graces and favors we ask during this Novena, if they be beneficial to our immortal souls, and the souls for which we pray: *(Mention your request).*

You know, Mary, how often our souls have been the sanctuaries of your Son Who hates iniquity. Obtain for us then a deep hatred of sin and that purity of heart which will attach us to God alone so that our every thought, word, and deed may tend to His greater glory.

Obtain for us also a spirit of prayer and self-denial that we may recover by penance what we have lost by sin and at length attain to that blessed abode where you are the Queen of Angels and of People. Amen.

Act of Consecration

VIRGIN Mother of God, Mary Immaculate, we dedicate and consecrate ourselves to you under the title of Our Lady of the Miraculous Medal. May this Medal be a sure sign of your affection for us and a constant reminder of our duties toward you. Ever while wearing it, may we be blessed by your loving protection and preserved in the grace of your Son.

Most powerful Virgin, Mother of our Savior, keep us close to you every moment of our lives.

Obtain for us, your children, the grace of a happy death; so that, in union with you, we may enjoy the blessing of heaven forever. Amen.

Mary, conceived without sin, pray for us who have recourse to you. *(3 times.)*

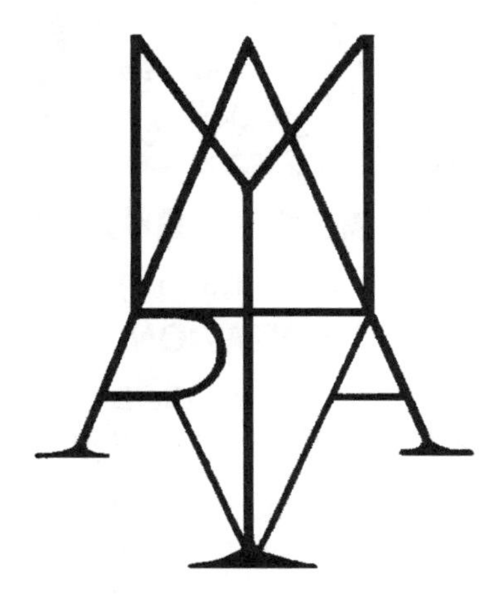

27. OUR LADY OF GUADALUPE

(December 12)

MEDITATION

ACCORDING to tradition the Blessed Virgin appeared to a fifty-five-year-old Aztec Indian Juan Diego, who was hurrying to Mass in Mexico City, on Saturday, December 9, 1531. She sent him to Bishop Zumaraga to ask that a church be built on the spot where she stood. She was at the same place that evening and Sunday evening to get the bishop's answer. After cross-questioning Juan, the bishop ordered him to ask for a sign from the lady who had said she was the Mother of God.

Mary spoke to Juan in these words: "Know and take heed, my dear little son, that I am the holy Mary, ever Virgin, Mother of the true God for Whom we live, the Creator of all the world, Maker of heaven and earth. I urgently desire that a church should be built here, to bear witness to my love, my compassion, my help and protection, For I am a merciful Mother to you and to all your people who love me and trust in me and invoke my help."

Our Lady would give the bishop a sign. She told Juan to go up to the rocks and gather roses. He knew it was neither the time nor the place for roses, but he obeyed. Gathering the roses into the long cloak worn by Mexican Indians, he returned to the Blessed Mother who arranged them. When he arrived at the bishop's home, Juan unfolded his cloak and the roses fell out. Startled to see the bishop and his attendants kneeling before him, he looked at the cloak and saw there the figure of the Virgin Mary, just as he had described her. The picture was venerated in the bishop's chapel and soon after carried in procession to the first church.

The picture that has aroused all this devotion is a representation of the Immaculate Conception, with the sun, moon, and stars, according to the text in the Book of Revelation. Mary, clothed in a blue robe dotted with stars, stands on the crescent moon. Underneath the crescent is a supporting Angel. The rays of the sun shoot out on all sides from behind the Blessed Mother.

In 1709, a rich and beautiful shrine was erected near Mexico City; in 1904, it was made a basilica and contains the picture. Pilgrimages have been made to this shrine almost uninterruptedly since 1531. A new and much larger basilica was recently completed. Twenty Popes favored the shrine and its tradition.

The apparition of Our Lady of Guadalupe is Mary's only recorded appearance in North America. Pope Pius XII said, "We are certain that so long as you—Our Lady of Guadalupe—are recognized as Queen and Mother, America and Mexico are saved." He proclaimed her the Patroness of the Americas. The United States was dedicated to the Immaculate Conception by the Third Plenary Council of Baltimore in 1846.

The Image of Our Lady of Guadalupe is the image of the Immaculate Conception. As patroness of Pan-American unity, Our Lady of Guadalupe influences her children to turn toward one another in common love for her and her beloved Son. Because of the close link between the Church in Mexico and the Church in the United States this feast is also celebrated in the United States on December 12.

THE WORD OF GOD

"I have chosen and sanctified this place, that my name may be there forever, and my eyes and my heart may be there perpetually." —2 Chr 7:16

"You are beautiful . . . , O My love, as comely as Jerusalem, as awe-inspiring as an army in battle array." —Song 6:4

"Who is she that comes forth like the morning rising, as beautiful as the moon, as bright as the sun, as awe-inspiring as an army in battle array?" —Song 6:10

NOVENA PRAYERS

Novena Prayer

OUR Lady of Guadalupe, according to your message in Mexico I venerate you as "the Virgin Mother of the true God for Whom we live, the Creator of all the world, Maker of heaven and earth." In spirit I kneel before your most holy Image which you miraculously imprinted upon the cloak of the Indian Juan Diego, and with the faith of the countless numbers of pilgrims who visit your shrine, I beg you for this favor: *(Mention your request).*

Remember, O Immaculate Virgin, the words you spoke to your devout client, "I am a merciful Mother to you and to all your people who love me and trust in me and invoke my help. I listen to their lamentations and solace all their sorrows and their sufferings." I beg you to be a merciful Mother to me, because I sincerely love you and trust in you and invoke your help.

I entreat you, Our Lady of Guadalupe, to grant my request, if this should be the Will of God, in order that I may "bear witness to your love, your compassion, your help and protection." Do not forsake me in my needs.

Our Lady of Guadalupe, pray for us. Hail Mary *(3 times).*

For the Church

OUR Lady of Guadalupe, mystical rose, make intercession for Holy Church, protect the Sovereign Pontiff, help all those who invoke you in their needs, and since you are the ever-Virgin Mary and Mother of the true God, obtain for us from your most holy Son the grace of keeping our faith, firm hope in the midst of the bitterness of life, burning charity, and the precious gift of final perseverance. Amen.

For Our Country

OUR Lady of the Americas, you have blessed our land with your gracious personal visit and numberless miracles, and have left us your own Image as the Immaculate Conception, "Patroness of the United States," and "the Woman clothed with the sun." Be pleased to protect our country from the dangers of war and communism. Help our citizens to serve God faithfully, to respect His holy laws, and finally to be eternally happy with Him in heaven.

Our Lady of Guadalupe, protectress of America, give us peace. Amen.

Prayer by Pope John Paul II

O IMMACULATE Virgin, Mother of the true God and Mother of the Church! You, who from this place reveal your clemency and your pity to all those who ask for your protection; hear the prayer that we address to you with filial trust, and present it to your Son Jesus, our sole Redeemer.

Mother of mercy, Teacher of hidden and silent sacrifice, to you, who come to meet us sinners, we dedicate on this day all our being and all our love. We also dedicate to you our life, our work, our joys, our infirmities and our sorrows.

Grant peace, justice, and prosperity to our people; for we entrust to your care all that we have and all that we are, Our Lady and Mother.

We wish to be entirely yours and to walk with you along the way of complete faithfulness to Jesus Christ in His Church: hold us always with your loving hand.

Virgin of Guadalupe, Mother of the Americas, we pray to you for all the Bishops, that they may lead the faithful along paths of intense Christian life, of love and humble service of God and souls.

Contemplate this immense harvest, and intercede with the Lord that He may instill a hunger for holiness in the whole People of God, and grant abundant vocations of priests and religious, strong in the faith and zealous dispensers of God's mysteries.

Grant to our homes the grace of loving and respecting life in its beginnings, with the same love with which you conceived in your womb the life of the Son of God.

Blessed Virgin Mary, Mother of Fair Love, protect our families, so that they may always be united, and bless the upbringing of our children.

Our hope, look upon us with compassion, teach us to go continually to Jesus and, if we fall, help us to rise again, to return to Him, by means of the confession of our faults and sins in the Sacrament of Penance, which gives peace to the soul. We beg you to grant us a great love for all the holy Sacraments, which are, as it were, the signs that your Son left us on earth.

Thus, Most Holy Mother, with the peace of God in our conscience, with our hearts free from evil and hatred, we will be able to bring to all true joy and true peace, which come to us from your Son, our Lord Jesus Christ, Who with God the Father and the Holy Spirit, lives and reigns forever. Amen.

Mexico, January 1979

Patroness of the Americas and Mexico

How kind you were, O Mary, to appear to an Indian convert in Mexico, leaving on his cloak as credential a permanent image of yourself. You thereby won many for Christ and naturally became the Patroness of Mexico and the Americas, and especially of the poor.

May more and more people through your intercession accept your dear Son as their Lord.

Prayer

GOD of power and mercy, You blessed the Americas at Tepeyac with the presence of the Virgin Mary at Guadalupe. May her prayers help all men and women to accept each other as brothers and sisters. Through Your justice present in our hearts may Your peace reign in the world. We ask this through our Lord Jesus Christ, Your Son, Who lives and reigns with You and the Holy Spirit, one God, forever and ever. Amen.

"Blessed be God in His Angels
and in His Saints."

Part Three

THE ANGELS AND SAINTS

MARCH—

28. SAINT JOHN OF GOD

(March 8)

Patron of Heart Patients

MEDITATION

JOHN was born in Portugal in 1495. He was a shepherd-boy until he was twenty-two years of age. For eighteen years he was a soldier in many parts of Europe. Even though he led a wild life, he loved the poor and the suffering.

John was over forty years old when he left the army in order to make up for his sins. He went back to Spain and rented a house. In it he gathered all the sick, the poor, and the homeless of the town of Granada. Often carrying them there on his own back, he washed them and dressed their sores, and begged food for them. He brought many sinners back to God.

Kind people began to help him in his work. The Order that he founded grew. It became known as the Hospitaller Order of Saint John of God. His motto was: "Labor without stopping; do all the good works you can while you still have the time."

After saving a man from drowning, John became very ill. On March 8, 1550, the nurses found him kneeling before a crucifix, his face resting on the feet of Jesus. The cause of his illness was overexhaustion. He died of a failing heart and is therefore honored as the patron of heart patients.

The feast of Saint John of God is celebrated on March 8.

THE WORD OF GOD

"This . . . is the fasting that I desire: share your bread with the hungry, shelter the needy and the homeless; clothe the naked when you see them, and do not turn your back on your own." —Isa 58:6-7

"Come, you who are blessed by My Father! Inherit the Kingdom prepared for you from the foundation of the world. . . . I was sick and you took care of Me."
—Mt 25:34, 36

"We must do the works of Him Who sent Me while it is day. Night is approaching when no one can work."
—Jn 9:4

NOVENA PRAYERS

Novena Prayer

SAINT John of God, I honor you as the patron of the sick, especially of those who are afflicted by heart disease. I choose you to be my patron and protector in my present need. I confidently place before you my earnest petition: *(Mention your request).*

I beg you to recommend my request to Mary, the Mother of Sorrows and Health of the Sick, that both Mary and you may present it to Jesus, the Divine Physician.

Saint John of God, I entrust my soul, my body, all my spiritual and temporal interests to you. To you I entrust my mind, that in all things it may be enlightened by faith, above all in accepting my cross as a blessing from God; my heart, that you may keep it pure and fill it with the love for Jesus and Mary that burned in yours; my will, that like yours, it may always be one with the Will of God.

Saint John of God, I honor you as the model of penitents, for you received the grace to give up a sinful life and to atone for our sins by untiring labors in behalf of the poor and sick. Obtain for me the grace from God to be truly sorry for my sins, to make atonement for them and never again offend God. Aid me in mastering my evil inclinations and temptations, and in avoiding all occasions of sin.

Through your intercession may I obtain the grace from Jesus and Mary to fulfill faithfully all the duties of my state of life and to practice those virtues which are needful for my salvation. Help me to belong to God and Our Lady in life and in death through perfect love. May my life, like yours, be spent in the untiring service of God and my neighbor.

I beg you to be with me in my last hour and pray for me. As you died kneeling before a crucifix, may I find strength, consolation and salvation in the Cross of my Redeemer, and through His tender mercy and the prayers of Our Lady, and through your intercession, attain to eternal life. Amen.

Prayer

GOD, You enabled Saint John, who was inflamed with love of You, to serve the sick, and by him You enriched Your Church with a new religious Order. Grant, through the help of his prayers and merits, that our vices may be healed by the fire of Your love, and that we may receive remedies that will help us reach eternal life. We ask this through Christ our Lord. Amen.

29. SAINT JOSEPH

(March 19; May 1)

Patron of the Universal Church

MEDITATION

SAINT Joseph is venerated as the husband of the Blessed Virgin Mary, the legal father of Jesus, and the head of the Holy Family. He was Mary's support and protector, a witness to her virginity, a consoler in her difficult vocation.

God comforted Joseph in a prophetic dream. He revealed to him in some measure the mystery of the Incarnation, the adorable Name of Jesus and His mission on earth. He removed every doubt from Joseph's mind and encouraged him to take to himself Mary for his wife. He freed him from worry and rewarded him with honors.

Joseph's sanctity was great to render him worthy of such a vocation. His holiness is measured by his close relation to Mary, his spotless Virgin-Spouse and to Jesus, his Divine Foster-Child.

His union with Mary is the closest that can exist, a union of heart with heart, a union of purest and holiest love. To what heights of sanctity must he have risen during this holy union on earth!

As the foster-father of Jesus, Joseph stands in close relation to the Son of God, the Fountain of all holiness. He surely has a greater share in his infinite sanctity than any other Saint, excepting Mary. Numberless are the graces and privileges connected with his exalted office.

We should love and honor him whom Jesus and His Mother love so tenderly. Through his intercession we can obtain the grace to love Jesus and Mary with some of that tenderness and devotedness with which he loves them.

Joseph served the Divine Child with a singular love. God gave him a heart filled with heavenly, supernatural love—a love far deeper and more powerful than any natural father's love could be.

Joseph served Jesus with great unselfishness, without any regard to self-interest, but not without sacrifices. He did not toil for himself, but he seemed to be an instrument intended for the benefit of others, to be put aside as soon as it had done its work, for he disappeared from the scene once the childhood of Jesus had passed.

Joseph's is a very special rank among the Saints of the Kingdom of God, because he was so much a part of the very life of the Word of God made Man. In his house at Nazareth and under his care the redemption of mankind was prepared. What he accomplished, he did also for those for whom Jesus was to give His life. He is not only a powerful and great Saint in the Kingdom of God but a benefactor of the whole of Christendom and mankind. His rank in the Kingdom of God, surpassing far in dignity and honor all the Angels and Saints, deserves our very special veneration, love, and gratitude.

THE WORD OF GOD

"Joseph, [Mary's] husband . . . was a just man."
—Mt 1:19

"He holds victory in store for the upright, He is the shield of those who walk blamelessly, for He guards the paths of the just, and protects the way of those faithful to Him."
—Prov 2:7-8

" 'Joseph, son of David, do not be afraid to receive Mary into your home as your wife. . . . She will give birth to a Son, and you shall name Him Jesus for He will save His people from their sins.' . . . When Joseph awoke he did as the Angel of the Lord had commanded him." —Mt 1:20-21, 24

"[Jesus] went down with them and came to Nazareth, and He was obedient to [Mary and Joseph]." —Lk 2:51

NOVENA PRAYERS

Novena Prayer

SAINT Joseph, you are the faithful protector and intercessor of all who love and venerate you. I have special confidence in you. You are powerful with God and will never abandon your faithful servants.

I humbly invoke you and commend myself, with all who are dear to me, to your intercession. By the love you have for Jesus and Mary, do not abandon me during life, and assist me at the hour of my death.

Glorious Saint Joseph, spouse of the immaculate Virgin, Foster-father of Jesus Christ, obtain for me a pure, humble, and charitable mind, and perfect resignation to the Divine Will. Be my guide, my father, and my model through life that I may merit to die as you did in the arms of Jesus and Mary.

Loving Saint Joseph, faithful follower of Jesus Christ, I raise my heart to you to implore your powerful intercession in obtaining from the Heart of Jesus all the graces necessary for my spiritual and temporal welfare, particularly the grace of a happy death, and the special grace I now implore: *(Mention your request).*

Guardian of the Word Incarnate, I am confident that your prayers in my behalf will be graciously heard before the throne of God.

Remember, Saint Joseph

REMEMBER, most pure spouse of Mary, ever Virgin, my loving protector, Saint Joseph, that no one ever had recourse to your protection or asked your aid without obtaining relief.

Confiding, therefore, in your goodness, I come before you and humbly implore you. Despise not my petitions, Foster-father of the Redeemer, but graciously receive them.

Consecration of the Family

JESUS, our most loving Redeemer, You came to enlighten the world with Your teaching and example. You willed to spend the greater part of Your life in humble obedience to Mary and Joseph in the poor home of Nazareth. In this way You sanctified that Family which was to be an example for all Christian families.

Jesus, Mary, Joseph! Graciously accept our family which we dedicate and consecrate to You. Be pleased to protect, guard, and keep it in sincere faith, in peace, and in the harmony of Christian charity. By conforming ourselves to the Divine model of Your Family, may we all attain to eternal happiness.

Mary, Mother of Jesus and our Mother, by your merciful intercession make this our humble offering acceptable to Jesus, and obtain for us graces and blessings.

Saint Joseph, most holy guardian of Jesus and Mary, help us by your prayers in all our spiritual and temporal needs so that we may praise Jesus, our Divine Savior, together with Mary and you for all eternity.

For the Church

GLORIOUS Saint Joseph, powerful protector of Holy Church, I implore your heavenly aid for the whole Church on earth, especially for the Holy Father and all bishops, priests, and religious.

Comfort the afflicted, console the dying, and convert sinners and heretics. Have pity on the poor souls in purgatory, especially on my own family, relatives, and friends. Obtain for them the speedy remission of their punishment, that with you and all the Saints and Angels they may praise and glorify the Blessed Trinity forever.

Prayer

GOD our Father, creator and ruler of the universe, in every age You call human beings to develop and use their gifts for the good of others. With Saint Joseph as our example and guide, help us to do the work You have asked and come to the rewards You have promised.

Inspired by the example of Saint Joseph, may our lives manifest Your love and may we rejoice forever in Your peace. Grant this through Christ our Lord. Amen.

Litany of Saint Joseph

LORD, have mercy *Christ, have mercy.*
Lord, have mercy.
Christ hear us.
Christ, graciously hear us.
God the Father of heaven, *have mercy on us.*
God the Son, Redeemer of the world,
God the Holy Spirit,
Holy Trinity, one God,
Holy Mary, pray for us.
Saint Joseph,*
Renowned offspring of David,
Light of patriarchs,
Spouse of the Mother of God,
Chaste guardian of the Virgin,
Foster-father of the Son of God,

* *Pray for us* is repeated after each invocation.

Diligent protector of Christ,
Head of the Holy Family,
Joseph most just,
Joseph most chaste,
Joseph most prudent,
Joseph most strong,
Joseph most obedient,
Joseph most faithful,
Mirror of patience,
Lover of poverty,
Model of artisans,
Glory of home life,
Guardian of virgins,
Pillar of families,
Solace of the wretched
Hope of the sick,
Patron of the dying,
Terror of demons,
Protector of Holy Church,

Lamb of God, You take away the sins of the world; *spare us, O Lord.*

Lamb of God, You take away the sins of the world; *graciously hear us, O Lord.*

Lamb of God, You take away the sins of the world; *have mercy on us.*

℣. He has made him the lord of His house,

℟. *And the ruler of His possessions.*

Prayer

LET us pray. O God, in Your ineffable providence You were pleased to choose Blessed Joseph to be the spouse of Your most holy Mother. Grant, we beg You, that we may be worthy to have him for our intercessor in heaven whom on earth we venerate as our Protector: You Who live and reign forever and ever. ℟. *Amen.*

—MAY—

30. SAINT PEREGRINE

(May 2)

Patron of Cancer Patients

MEDITATION

PEREGRINE was born in 1260 at Forli, Italy. He belonged to an anti-papal party. St. Philip Benizi was sent by the Pope to preach peace at Forli. Peregrine knocked down the holy man by striking him on the face. The Saint's only reply was to pray for the youth. This impressed Peregrine, and he begged forgiveness on his knees.

Our Lady appeared to Peregrine and told him to go to Siena, where he was received into the Order of the Servants of Mary by Saint Philip himself.

Peregrine was to have his foot cut off because of a spreading cancer. While spending the night before the operation in prayer, he fell asleep before the image of the crucified Savior. In a dream, Christ seemed to stretch out His hand from the Cross and touch his diseased foot. On awakening he was completely cured.

For sixty-two years Peregrine lived a life of penance and prayer as a saintly priest. He died in 1345. He was chosen by the Church to be the patron of those suffering from running sores and cancer. Four hundred years after burial, the body of "the Cancer Saint" was found to be incorrupt. He is invoked as the patron of cancer patients. His feast is celebrated on May 2.

THE WORD OF GOD

"Through Christ you have been granted the privilege not only to believe in Him but also to suffer for Him."

—Phil 1:29

"You will weep and mourn while the world rejoices. You will be sorrowful, but your grief will turn into joy."

—Jn 16:20

"By standing firm you will gain life." —Lk 21:19

NOVENA PRAYERS

Novena Prayer

SAINT Peregrine, whom Holy Mother Church has declared patron of those suffering from running sores and cancer, I confidently turn to you for aid in my present need: *(Mention your request).*

Lest I lose confidence, I beg your kind intercession. Plead with Mary, the Mother of Sorrows, whom you loved so tenderly and in union with whom you have suffered the pains of cancer, that she may help me with her all-powerful prayers and consolation.

Obtain for me the strength to accept my trials from the loving hand of God with patience and resignation. May suffering lead me to a better life and enable me to atone for my own sins and the sins of the world.

Saint Peregrine, help me to imitate you in bearing whatever cross God may permit to come to me, uniting myself with Jesus Crucified and the Mother of Sorrows. I offer my sufferings to God with all the love of my heart, for His glory and the salvation of souls, especially my own. Amen.

Prayer

GOD, graciously hear the prayers which I present to You in honor of Saint Peregrine, Your beloved servant and devoted friend of Jesus Crucified and Our Mother of Sorrows, so that I may receive help in my needs through the intercession of him whose life had been so pleasing to You.

You filled Saint Peregrine with the spirit of compassion. Grant that by practicing works of charity I may deserve to be numbered among the elect in Your Kingdom. I ask this through Christ our Lord. Amen.

31. SAINT DYMPHNA

(May 15)

Patron of the Nervous and Emotionally Disturbed

MEDITATION

SAINT Dymphna was born in the seventh century. Her father, Damon, a chieftain of great wealth and power, was a pagan. Her mother was a very beautiful and devout Christian.

Dymphna was fourteen when her mother died. Damon is said to have been afflicted with a mental illness, brought on by his grief. He sent messengers throughout his own and other lands to find some woman of noble birth, resembling his wife, who would be willing to marry him. When none could be found his evil advisers told him to marry his own daughter. Dymphna fled from her castle together with Saint Gerebran, her confessor, and two other friends.

Damon found them in Belgium. He gave orders that the priest's head be cut off. Then he tried to persuade his daughter to return to Ireland with him. When she refused, he drew his sword and struck off her head. She was then only fifteen years of age.

Dymphna received the crown of martyrdom in defense of her purity about the year 620. She is the patron of those suffering from nervous and mental afflictions. Many miracles have taken place at her shrine, built on the spot where she was buried in Gheel, Belgium. Her feast is celebrated on May 15.

THE WORD OF GOD

"Those who believe . . . will cast out demons in My Name. . . . The sick upon whom they lay their hands will get well." —Mk 16:17-18

"He will deliver you from the snare of the hunter and from the pestilence that lays waste." —Ps 91:3

"Those who are planted in the house of the Lord will flourish in the courts of our God." —Ps 92:14

NOVENA PRAYERS

Novena Prayer

SAINT Dymphna, a great wonderworker in every affliction of mind and body, I humbly implore your powerful intercession with Jesus through Mary, the Health of the Sick.

You are filled with love and compassion for the thousands of patients brought to your shrine for centuries, and for those who cannot come to your shrine but invoke you in their own homes or in hospitals. Show the same love and compassion toward me, your faithful client. The many miracles and cures which have been wrought through your intercession give me great confidence that you will help me in my present need: *(Mention your request).*

I am confident of obtaining my request, if it is for the greater glory of God and the good of my soul. For the sake of Jesus and Mary, whom you loved so earnestly, and for whom you offered your life in martyrdom, grant my prayer.

Saint Dymphna, young and beautiful, innocent and pure, help me to imitate your love of purity. You chose to be martyred by your own father's sword rather than consent to sin. Give me strength and courage in fighting off the temptations of the world and evil desires.

As you have given all the love of your heart to Jesus, help me to love God with my whole heart and serve Him faithfully. As you bore the persecution of your father and the sufferings of an exile so patiently, obtain for me the patience I need to accept the trials of my life with loving resignation to the will of God.

Saint Dymphna, through your glorious martyrdom for the love of Christ, help me to be loyal to my faith and my God as long as I live. And when the hour of my own death comes, stand at my side and pray for me that I may at last merit the eternal crown of glory in God's Kingdom.

Good Saint Dymphna, I beg you to recommend my request to Mary, the Health of the Sick and Comforter of the Afflicted, that both Mary and you may present it to Jesus, the Divine Physician.

Prayer

O GOD, You gave Saint Dymphna to Your Church as a model of all virtues, especially holy purity, and willed that she should seal her faith with her innocent blood and perform numerous miracles. Grant that we who honor her as patroness of those afflicted with nervous and mental illness may continue to enjoy her powerful intercession and protection and attain eternal life. We ask this through Christ our Lord. Amen.

32. SAINT RITA

(May 22)

Saint of the Impossible

MEDITATION

SAINT Rita might he described as the Saint with family troubles: she was in a very real sense the victim of an unhappy marriage. She was born in 1381 of an ordinary peasant family in central Italy.

When Rita at an early age showed an inclination for convent life and asked permission of her parents to follow that vocation, they would not hear of it. Instead, as Rita reached the age of fifteen, they arranged a marriage for her, according to the custom of that day, with a man of their own choice. And Rita, with a sad heart, yet feeling that to obey her parents in this matter was to obey God, settled down in her new vocation, resolved to be a good wife that thus she might save and sanctify her soul.

Rita's husband was a man of violent temper, which developed into brutality. He often kicked and struck his young wife for no other reason perhaps than that he was angry for losing at gambling. Rita's husband was guilty of open infidelity.

Two sons were born to them in the early years of their married life. Although Rita did her best to train them and educate them to the knowledge and love of God, their father delighted in teaching them his own evil ways.

One night her husband was stabbed by an enemy he made as a result of his violent way of life. Before he died, he came to himself, and showed every sign of repentance for his evil life, which surely was the result of Rita's prayers.

The boys died soon after at a very early age. "Only let them die in Your grace, O Lord," she prayed. Her prayer was heard. Both on their deathbeds had time to repent and to receive the Sacraments.

For eighteen years Rita bore heroically the troubles of her married life. Left alone in the world, she soon sought admission into a nearby Augustinian convent. But her suffering was not ended.

When Rita was about sixty years old, a small wound appeared on her forehead, as though a thorn from Christ's crown of thorns had penetrated her own flesh. For the last sixteen years of life, this mystic of the Cross patiently and lovingly bore that external and painful sign of stigmatization and union with Christ. Since it was accompanied by a wasting sickness, Rita had to be taken care of in an isolated part of her convent.

At last, with perfect resignation to God's Will, she died, on May 22, 1457, acclaimed a Saint by all, and was soon officially declared a Saint by the Church. Her feast is celebrated on May 22.

THE WORD OF GOD

"I have come to set a man against his father, a daughter against her mother. Your enemies will be the members of your own household." —Mt 10:35-36

"As long as you remain in Me and I in you, you bear much fruit, but apart from Me you can do nothing." —Jn 15:5

"I do not wish to boast of anything but the Cross of our Lord Jesus Christ. Through it, the world has been crucified to me and I to the world." —Gal 6:14

NOVENA PRAYERS

Prayer to the Heavenly Father

HEAVENLY Father, rewarder of the humble, You blessed Saint Rita with charity and patience. You kept her faithful to the pattern of poverty and humility of Your Son during the years of her married life and especially in the convent where she served You for the rest of her life.

In Saint Rita You give us an example of the Gospel lived to perfection, for You called her to seek Your Kingdom in this world by striving to live in perfect charity. In her life You teach us that the commandments of heaven are summarized in love of You and love of others.

May the prayers of Saint Rita help me and her example inspire me to carry my cross and to love You always. Pour upon me the spirit of wisdom and love with which You filled Your servant, so that I may serve You faithfully and reach eternal life. I ask this through Christ our Lord. Amen.

Novena Prayer

SAINT Rita, God gave you to us as an example of charity and patience, and offered you a share in the Passion of His Son. I thank Him for the many blessings He bestowed upon you during your lifetime, especially during your unhappy marriage and during the illness you suffered in the convent.

May your example encourage me to carry my own Cross patiently and to live a holier life. By serving God as you did, may I please Him with my faith and my actions.

I fail because of my weakness. Pray to God for me that He may restore me to His love through His grace and help me on my way to salvation.

In your kindness hear my prayer and ask God to grant me this particular request if it be His Will: *(Mention your request).*

May your prayers help me to live in fidelity to my calling as you did and bring me to the deeper love of God and my neighbor until I reach eternal life in heaven. Amen.

Alternative Novena Prayer

HOLY Patroness of those in need, Saint Rita, your pleadings before your Divine Lord are irresistible. For your lavishness in granting favors you have been called the "Advocate of the Hopeless" and even of the "Impossible."

You are so humble, so mortified, so patient, and so compassionate in love for your crucified Jesus that you can obtain from Him anything you ask. Therefore, all confidently have recourse to you in the hope of comfort or relief.

Be propitious toward your suppliants and show your power with God in their behalf. Be lavish of your favors now as you have been in so many wonderful cases for the greater glory of God, the spread of your devotion, and the consolation of those who trust in you. We promise, if our petition be granted, to glorify you by making known your favor, and to bless you and sing your praises forever. Relying then on your merits and power before the Sacred Heart of Jesus, we ask of you: *(Mention your request).*

Prayer

O GOD, in Your infinite tenderness You have been pleased to regard the prayer of Your servant Rita, and to grant to her supplication that which is impossible to human foresight, skill, and effort, in reward for her compassionate love and firm reliance on Your promises.

Have pity on our adversities and comfort us in our calamities, that unbelievers may know that You are the recompense of the humble, the defense of the helpless, and the strength of those who trust in You. Grant this in the Name of Jesus the Lord.

—JUNE—

33. SAINT ANTHONY OF PADUA

(June 13)

The Wonderworker

MEDITATION

ANTHONY'S parents were rich and wanted him to be a great nobleman. But he wanted to be poor for the sake of Christ, so he became a Franciscan.

Anthony was a great preacher. He was sent out as a missionary and preached in many cities in Italy and France. He brought many sinners back to God, mostly by his good example.

It is said that when Anthony was praying in his room, the Infant Jesus appeared to him, put His little arms around his neck, and kissed him. This wonderful favor was given to Anthony because he kept his soul free from even the smallest sin and because he loved Jesus very much.

When Anthony became ill he went to a monastery outside of Padua, where he died at the age of only thirty-six on June 13, 1231. Thirty-two years after his death his remains were brought to Padua. All the flesh except the tongue had been consumed by corruption. Many miracles took place after his death. Even today he is called the "Wonderworker." His feast is celebrated on June 13.

Saint Anthony is one of the most popular of Saints. He is called the "Saint of the Whole World" because the faithful of the whole world love him. During the past seven hundred years, millions have been attracted to this great Franciscan Wonderworker.

Another Franciscan, Saint Bonaventure, says, "Ask the Wonderworker with confidence, and he will obtain what you seek."

THE WORD OF GOD

"The Spirit of the Lord is upon Me. He has anointed Me to bring the Good News to the poor." —Lk 4:18

"I proclaim Your righteousness in the great assembly. . . I have spoken of Your faithfulness and Your salvation."
—Ps 40:10-11

"The tongue of the righteous is like choice silver. . . . The lips of the righteous nourish a multitude."
—Prov 10:20-21

NOVENA PRAYERS

Novena Prayer

SAINT Anthony, glorious for the fame of your miracles, obtain for me from God's mercy this favor that I desire: *(Mention your request).*

Since you were so gracious to poor sinners, do not regard my lack of virtue but consider the glory of God which will be exalted once more through you by the granting of the petition that I now earnestly present to you.

Glorious Wonderworker, Saint Anthony, father of the poor and comforter of the afflicted, I ask for your help. You have come to my aid with such loving care and have comforted me so generously. I offer you my heartfelt thanks.

Accept this offering of my devotion and love and with it my earnest promise which I now renew, to live always in the love of God and my neighbor. Continue to shield me graciously with your protection, and obtain for me the grace of being able one day to enter the Kingdom of heaven, there to praise with you the everlasting mercies of God. Amen.

Litany of Saint Anthony

(For Private Devotion)

LORD, have mercy. *Christ, have mercy.*
Lord, have mercy.
Christ, hear us.
Christ, graciously hear us.
Holy Mary, pray for us.
Saint Francis,*
Saint Anthony of Padua,
Glory of the Order of Friars Minor,
Martyr in desiring to die for Christ,
Pillar of the Church,
Worthy priest of God,
Apostolic preacher,
Teacher of truth,

* *Pray for us* is repeated after each invocation down to *Be merciful to us.*

Conqueror of heretics,
Terror of evil spirits,
Comforter of the afflicted,
Helper in necessities,
Guide of the erring,
Restorer of lost things,
Chosen intercessor,
Continuous worker of miracles,
Be merciful to us, *spare us, O Lord.*
Be merciful to us, *hear us, O Lord.*
From all evil, *deliver us, O Lord.*
From all sin,**
From all dangers of body and soul,
From the snares of the devil,
From pestilence, famine, and war,
From eternal death,
Through the merits of Saint Anthony,
Through his zeal for the conversion of sinners,
Through his desire for the crown of martyrdom,
Through his fatigues and labors,
Through his preaching and teaching,
Through his penitential tears,
Through his patience and humility,
Through his glorious death,
Through the number of his prodigies,
In the day of judgment,
We sinners, *we beseech You, hear us,*
That You would bring us to true penance,***
That You would grant us patience in our trials,
That You would assist us in our necessities,
That You would hear our prayers and petitions,
That You would kindle the fires of Divine love within us,
That You would grant us the protection and intercession of Saint Anthony,

** *Deliver us, O Lord* is repeated after each invocation down to *In the day of judgment.*

*** *We beseech you, hear us,* is repeated after each invocation down to Son of God.

Son of God,

Lamb of God, You take away the sins of the world; *spare us, O Lord.*

Lamb of God, You take away the sins of the world; *graciously hear us, O Lord.*

Lamb of God, You take away the sins of the world; *have mercy on us.*

Christ, hear us.

Christ, graciously hear us.

℣. Pray for us, O blessed Saint Anthony.

℟. *That we may be made worthy of the promises of Christ.*

Prayer

LET us pray. Almighty and eternal God, You glorified Your faithful confessor Anthony with the perpetual gift of working miracles. Grant that what we confidently seek through his merits we may surely receive by his intercession. We ask this in the Name of Jesus the Lord. ℟. *Amen.*

—JULY—

34. SAINT ANNE

(July 26)

Patroness of Mothers

MEDITATION

THE *dignity* of Saint Anne is great because her daughter was Mary, predestined from all eternity to be the Mother of God, sanctified in her conception, the undefiled Virgin, the Mediatrix of all graces. Her Grandson was the Son of God made Man, the Messiah, the Expected of Nations. Mary is not only the joy and crown, but the foundation for all the glory and power of her mother.

Saint Anne's *sanctity* is so great because of the many graces that God has bestowed upon her. Her very name signifies "grace." God prepared her with magnificent gifts and graces. As the works of God are perfect, it was natural to expect that He should make her a worthy mother of the most pure creature who was superior in sanctity to all creatures and inferior only to God.

Saint Anne was zealous in performing good works and striving for virtue. She loved God sincerely, and was resigned to His holy Will in all sufferings, such as her sterility during twenty years as tradition suggests. As a wife and mother, she was faithful in fulfilling the duties required of her toward her husband and her loving daughter Mary.

The *power* of Saint Anne's intercession is very great. She is not only a Saint and a friend of God but also the grandmother of Jesus according to the flesh.

The Blessed Trinity will grant her petitions: the Father for Whom she bore, nursed, and trained His favored daughter; the Son, to Whom she gave a mother; the Holy Spirit, Whose bride she educated with such great care.

This favored Saint ranks high in merit and glory, near to the Word Incarnate and to His most holy Mother. Certainly, then, Saint Anne has great power with God. The mother of the Queen of heaven, who is all-powerful through her intercession and the Mother of mercy, is likewise full of power and mercy.

We nave every reason to choose Saint Anne as our intercessor before God. As grandmother of Jesus Christ, our Brother according to the flesh, she is also our grandmother and loves us, her grandchildren. She loves us with a great love because her Grandson Jesus died for our souls and Mary, her daughter, became our Mother beneath the Cross. She must love us sincerely because of the two Persons whom she loved most in her life, Jesus and Mary. If her love is so great, her intercession is also great. We should, therefore, go to her with great confidence in our needs. This would certainly please Jesus and Mary who loved her so dearly.

The feast of Saint Anne is celebrated on July 26.

THE WORD OF GOD

"[Anna] was continually in the Temple, worshiping day and night."
—Lk 2:37

"[She] will receive a blessing from the Lord and vindication from God [her] Savior."
—Ps 24:5

"Blessed are your eyes because they see, and your ears because they hear. . . . Many Prophets and holy people longed to see what you see but did not see it."
—Mt 13:16-17

NOVENA PRAYERS

Novena Prayer

GLORIOUS Saint Anne, I desire to honor you with a special devotion. I choose you, after the Blessed Virgin, as my spiritual mother and protectress. To you I entrust my soul and my body, all my spiritual and temporal interests, as well as those of my family.

To you I consecrate my mind, that in all things it may be enlightened by faith; my heart, that you may keep it pure and fill it with love for Jesus, Mary, Joseph, and yourself; my will, that like yours, it may always be one with the Will of God.

Good Saint Anne, filled with love for those who invoke you and with compassion for those who suffer, I confidently place before you my earnest petition: *(Mention your request).*

I beg you to recommend my petition to your daughter, the Blessed Virgin Mary, that both Mary and you may present it to Jesus. Through your earnest prayers may my request be granted. But if what I ask for should not be according to the Will of God, obtain for me that which will be for the greater benefit of my soul. By the power and the grace with which God has blessed you, extend to me your helping hand.

But most of all, merciful Saint Anne, I beg you to help me to master my evil inclinations and temptations, and to avoid all occasions of sin. Obtain for me the grace of never offending God, of fulfilling faithfully all the duties of my state of life, and of practicing all those virtues that are needful for my salvation.

Like you, may I belong to God in life and in death through perfect love. And after having loved and honored you on earth as a truly devoted child, may I, through your prayers, have the privilege of loving and honoring you in heaven with the Angels and Saints throughout eternity.

Good Saint Anne, mother of her who is our life, our sweetness and our hope, pray to her for me and obtain my request.

Memorare to Saint Anne

REMEMBER, good Saint Anne, whose name means grace and mercy, that never was it known that anyone who fled to your protection, implored your help or sought your intercession, was left unaided.

Inspired with this confidence, I come before you, sinful and sorrowful. Holy mother of the Immaculate Virgin Mary and loving grandmother of the Savior, do not reject my appeal, but hear me and answer my prayer. Amen.

Prayer to Saint Joachim and Saint Anne

GREAT and glorious patriarch, Saint Joachim, and good Saint Anne, what joy is mine when I consider that you were chosen among all God's holy ones to assist in the fulfillment of the mysteries of God, and to enrich our earth with the great Mother of God, Mary most holy. By this singular privilege, you have become most powerful with both the Mother and her Son, so as to be able to obtain for us the graces that are needful to us.

With great confidence I have recourse to your mighty protection, and I commend to you all my needs, both spiritual and temporal, and those of my family. Especially do I entrust to your keeping the particular favor that I desire and look for from your intercession.

And since you were a perfect pattern of the interior life, obtain for me the grace to pray earnestly, and never to set my heart on the passing goods of this life. Give me a lively and enduring love for Jesus and Mary. Obtain for me also a sincere devotion and obedience to

Holy Church and the sovereign pontiff who rules over her, in order that I may live and die in faith and hope and perfect charity. Let me ever invoke the holy Names of Jesus and Mary. And may I thus be saved.

Litany in Honor of Saint Anne

(For Private Devotion)

LORD, have mercy *Christ, have mercy.*
Lord, have mercy.
Christ, hear us.
Christ, graciously hear us.
God the Father of heaven, *have mercy on us.*
God, the Son, Redeemer of the world,*
God, the Holy Spirit,
Holy Trinity, one God,
Saint Anne, *pray for us.*
Offspring of the royal race of David,**
Daughter of the Patriarchs,
Faithful spouse of Saint Joachim,
Mother of Mary, the Virgin Mother of God,
Gentle mother of the Queen of heaven,
Grandmother of Our Savior,
Beloved of Jesus, Mary, and Joseph,
Instrument of the Holy Spirit,
Richly endowed with God's grace,
Example of piety and patience in suffering,
Mirror of obedience,
Ideal of pure womanhood,
Protectress of virgins,
Model of Christian mothers,
Protectress of the married,
Guardian of children,
Support of Christian family life,
Help of the Church,
Mother of mercy,
Mother of confidence,
Friend of the poor,
Example of widows,
Health of the sick,

Have mercy on us is repeated for these next three invocations.
***Pray for us* is repeated after each invocation.

Cure of those who suffer from disease,
Mother of the infirm,
Light of the blind,
Speech of those who cannot speak,
Hearing of the deaf,
Consolation of the afflicted,
Comforter of the oppressed,
Joy of the Angels and Saints,
Refuge of sinners,
Harbor of salvation,
Patroness of a happy death,
Help of all who have recourse to you,

Lamb of God, You take away the sins of the world; *spare us, O Lord*
Lamb of God, You take away the sins of the world; *graciously hear us, O Lord.*
Lamb of God, You take away the sins of the world; have *mercy on us.*

℣. Pray for us, good Saint Anne.
℟. *That we may be made worthy of the promises of Christ.*

Prayer

LET us pray. Almighty and eternal God, You were pleased to choose Saint Anne to be the mother of the Mother of Your loving Son. Grant, we pray, that we who confidently honor her may through her prayers attain to everlasting life. We ask this through Jesus Christ our Lord. ℟. *Amen.*

—AUGUST—

35. SAINT ALPHONSUS LIGUORI

(August 1)

Patron of Arthritis Patients

MEDITATION

ALPHONSUS was born near Naples in Italy, in 1696, of a noble Italian family. At nineteen he began to practice law and became one of the leading lawyers in Naples. He never went to the law courts without having first attended Mass. He then made up his mind to become a priest.

Alphonsus preached missions. Large crowds came to hear him. He often visited the sick. He wrote many spiritual books. He organized a community of priests in honor of the Most Holy Redeemer, the Redemptorists, who preach parish missions.

The Pope commanded Alphonsus to become a bishop. During the thirteen years that he was bishop his health was poor. An attack of rheumatism left him a cripple for the rest of his life. His head was so badly bent that his chin pressed against his chest. He suffered intense pain. Arthritis had gripped his wrists and spine. He continued handling details of work from his bed. Because of his arthritic condition he is invoked as the patron of those who suffer with the disease of arthritis.

Alphonsus had a great love for the Blessed Sacrament and Our Lady. He wrote the *Glories of Mary* and *Visits to the Blessed Sacrament*. He was given the title of "Doctor of the Church."

Alphonsus died on August 1, 1787. His feast is celebrated on August 1.

THE WORD OF GOD

"How I love Your law, O Lord! I meditate on it all day long." —Ps 119:97

"Every teacher of the law who has been instructed about the Kingdom of God is like the owner of a house who brings forth from his storeroom new treasures as well as old." —Mt 13:52

"[He] is the faithful and wise servant whom his Master has put in charge of His household to give its members their food at the proper time." —Mt 24:45

NOVENA PRAYERS

Novena Prayer

GLORIOUS Saint Alphonsus, Bishop and Doctor of the Church, devoted servant of our Lord and loving child of Mary, I invoke you as a Saint in heaven. I give myself to your protection that you may always be my father, my protector, and my guide in the way of holiness and salvation. Aid me in observing the duties of my state of life. Obtain for me great purity of heart and a fervent love of the interior life after your own example.

Great lover of the Blessed Sacrament and the Passion of Jesus Christ, teach me to love Holy Mass and Holy Communion as the source of grace and holiness. Give me a tender devotion to the Passion of my Redeemer.

Promoter of the truth of Christ in your preaching and writing, give me a greater knowledge and appreciation of the Divine truths.

Gentle father of the poor and sinners, help me to imitate your charity toward others in word and deed.

Consoler of the suffering, help me to bear my daily cross patiently in imitation of your own patience in your long and painful illness and to resign myself to the Will of God.

Good Shepherd of the flock of Christ, obtain for me the grace of being a true child of Holy Mother Church.

Saint Alphonsus, I humbly implore your powerful intercession for obtaining from the Heart of Jesus all the graces necessary for my spiritual and temporal welfare. I recommend to you in particular this favor: *(Mention your request)*.

I have great confidence in your prayers. I earnestly trust that if it is God's holy Will, my petition will be granted through your intercession for me at the throne of God.

Saint Alphonsus, pray for me and for those I love. I beg of you, by your love for Jesus and Mary, do not abandon us in our needs. May we experience the peace and joy of your holy death. Amen.

Prayer

HEAVENLY Father, You continually build up Your Church by the lives of Your Saints. Give us grace to follow Saint Alphonsus in his loving concern for the salvation of people and so come to share his reward in heaven. Walking in the footsteps of this devoted servant of Yours, may we be consumed with zeal for souls and attain the reward he enjoys in Your Kingdom. We ask this through Christ our Lord. Amen.

—SEPTEMBER—

36. SAINT MICHAEL THE ARCHANGEL

(September 29)

MEDITATION

SAINT Michael is *the protector of the Church.* The Church, as far back as the fourth century, has paid special honor to the glorious Archangel Michael, whom in her liturgy she invokes as "Prince of the heavenly host." His name is the war cry with which he smote Lucifer and his proud followers and cast them out of heaven into the depths of hell. His name means: "Who is like God?"

The battle is still being waged in the world. God gave us through His Son Jesus Christ, a Church to teach, rule, and sanctify us, and lead us to His Kingdom in heaven. God wants us to become holy, for our holiness means glory to God and the triumph of His Church. But revolt against God and His Church is set against this Divine triumph and glory. Satan and his devils attack God and His Church in religious, social, political, economic, and educational areas of life.

Michael has always been the warrior Angel fighting Lucifer in heaven, fighting the enemies of God's chosen people of old, and now fighting the enemies of the Catholic Church. He is ever fighting, resisting, and overcoming the power of darkness.

When the foundation of society is shaken because of a lack of faith in God, there is need to revive veneration to Saint Michael and to live according to the spirit that reigns in him, the spirit of God.

Saint Michael is the protector of the faithful. Special excellence is attached to Saint Michael's intercession because of his position in the Mystical Body of Christ. Although it is true that all the Angels in heaven are members of this same body, yet Saint Michael, being the prince of the heavenly host and patron and protector of the Church, has a unique place in it. He occupies a special place of honor and patronage over the members of the Mystical Body of Christ. God and the Church appointed him for such a patronage.

The Church urges us to seek the patronage of Saint Michael against all evils, but especially against the evils that threaten the salvation of our soul. We must meet the attacks of the enemy by building up our own spiritual life, our power and resistance, and also by using a spiritual remedy against the enemies of our spiritual life and happiness. God offers us many means: grace, infused virtues of faith, hope, and love, gifts of the Holy Spirit, Divine Revelation, the Sacraments, and prayer. He also gives us Angels and Saints like Saint Michael to protect and assist us.

The principal work of Saint Michael is to wage relentless warfare against Satan and his forces of evil, that he may prevent the eternal loss of souls, which were created by God and redeemed by the Passion and Death of His Divine Son. We must follow the standard-bearer of God's armies.

But the Church also urges us to seek the patronage of Saint Michael in all the needs of soul and body. He prays for those who seek his assistance. He knows well our great needs and the great dangers that surround us. He who loves God and His people with an intense love cannot but be mighty in his intercession.

Saint Michael renders every type of assistance to his clients on earth. This is proved by the widespread devotion to him and the various reasons and needs for which he has always been invoked almost since the foundation of the Church. He obtains both spiritual and material benefits and overcomes various kinds of evils detrimental to the soul and to the body.

We should try to cultivate a personal devotion to Saint Michael in our daily life. Angels are given us by Divine Providence to help us, especially spiritually, but we must be willing to let them work their good in us. We constantly need heavenly assistance to grow in spiritual life, in grace, in the love of God and our neighbor. We should entrust ourselves and our family to his care, and invoke his help frequently in our needs and problems. Especially at the hour of death we will find him our support and consolation and our defense against the enemies of our soul.

The feast of Saints Michael, Gabriel, and Raphael is celebrated on September 29.

THE WORD OF GOD

"The Archangel Michael . . . did not dare to denounce [the devil] in the language of abuse. He just said, 'May the Lord chastise you.' " —Jude 9

"In all this, there is no one to offer me support except Michael, Your Prince, I rely on him to be my reinforcement and my buckler." —Dan 11:1-2

"Michael and his Angels fought against the dragon. . . . The primeval serpent known as the devil or Satan, who led the whole world astray, was cast down." —Rev 12:7-9

NOVENA PRAYERS

Novena Prayer

SAINT Michael the Archangel, loyal champion of God and His people, I turn to you with confidence and seek your powerful intercession. For the love of God, Who made you so glorious in grace and power, and for the love of the Mother of Jesus, the Queen of the Angels, be pleased to hear my prayer. You know the value of my soul in the eyes of God. May no stain of evil ever disfigure its beauty. Help me to conquer the evil spirit who tempts me. I desire to imitate your loyalty to God and Holy Mother Church and your great love for God and people. And since you are God's messenger for the care of His people, I entrust to you this special request: *(Mention your request)*.

Saint Michael, since you are, by the Will of the Creator, the powerful intercessor of Christians, I have great confidence in your prayers. I earnestly trust that if it is God's holy Will, my petition will be granted.

Pray for me, Saint Michael, and also for those I love. Protect us in all dangers of body and soul. Help us in our daily needs. Through your powerful intercession, may we live a holy life, die a happy death, and reach heaven where we may praise and love God with you forever. Amen.

Consecration

SAINT Michael the Archangel, invincible prince of the angelic hosts and glorious protector of the Universal Church, I greet you and praise you for that splendor with which God has adorned you so richly. I thank God for the great graces He has bestowed upon you, especially to remain faithful when Lucifer and his followers rebelled, and to battle victoriously for the honor of God and the Divinity of the Son of Man.

Saint Michael, I consecrate to you my soul and body. I choose you as my patron and protector and entrust the salvation of my soul to your care. Be the guardian of my obligation as a child of God and of the Catholic Church as again I renounce Satan, his works, and his empty promises.

Assist me by your powerful intercession in the fulfillment of these sacred promises, so that imitating your courage and loyalty to God, and trusting in your kind help and protection, I may be victorious over the enemies of my soul and be united with God in heaven forever. Amen.

Prayer

SAINT Michael the Archangel, defend us in battle, be our protection against the wickedness and snares of the devil; may God rebuke him, we humbly pray; and do you, O Prince of the heavenly host, by the power of God, thrust into hell Satan and all evil spirits who wander through the world for the ruin of souls. Amen.

Saint Michael the Archangel, defend us in the battle, that we may not perish in the fearful judgment.

Saint Michael, first champion of the Kingship of Christ, pray for us.

God our Father, in a wonderful way You guide the work of Angels and human beings. May those who serve You constantly in heaven keep our lives safe from all harm on earth. Grant this through Christ our Lord. Amen.

Litany in Honor of Saint Michael

(For Private Devotion)

LORD, have mercy.
Christ, have mercy.
Lord, have mercy.
Christ, hear us.
Christ, graciously hear us.
God the Father of heaven,
have mercy on us.
God the Son, Redeemer of the world,
God the Holy Spirit,
Holy Trinity, one God,
Holy Mary, Queen of the Angels, *pray for us.*
Saint Michael, the Archangel,*
Most glorious attendant of the Triune Divinity,
Standing at the right of the altar of incense,
Ambassador of Paradise,
Glorious Prince of the heavenly armies,

* *Pray for us* is repeated after each invocation.

Leader of the angelic hosts,
The standard-bearer of God's armies,
Defender of Divine glory,
First defender of the Kingship of Christ,
Strength of God,
Invincible prince and warrior,
Angel of Peace,
Guide of Christ,
Guardian of the Christian Faith,
Champion of God's people,
Guardian Angel of the Eucharist,
Defender of the Church,
Protector of the Sovereign Pontiff,
Angel of Catholic apostolic work,
Powerful intercessor of Christians,
Brave defender of those who hope in God,
Guardian of our souls and bodies,
Healer of the sick,
Help of those in their agony,
Consoler of the souls in purgatory,
God's messenger for the souls of the just,
Terror of the evil spirits,
Victorious in battle against evil,
Guardian and Patron of the universal Church
Lamb of God, You take away the sins of the world; *spare us, O Lord.*
Lamb of God, You take away the sins of the world; *graciously hear us, O Lord*
Lamb of God, You take away the sins of the world; *have mercy on us.*

℣. Pray for us, O glorious Saint Michael,
℟. *That we may be made worthy of the promises of Christ.*

LET us pray. Relying, Lord, upon the intercession of Your blessed Archangel Michael, we humbly beg of You, that the Sacrament of the Eucharist that we have received may make our souls holy and pleasing to You. We ask this through Christ our Lord. ℟. *Amen.*

37. SAINT GABRIEL THE ARCHANGEL

(September 29)

MEDITATION

IN the New Testament the Angel Gabriel foretold the birth of the Precursor, John the Baptist. He appeared to Zechariah and announced John's task and office. He also foretold John's holiness and virtues, and the success of his life and mission. He said, "I am Gabriel. I stand in the presence of God, and I have been sent to speak to you and to convey to you this good news" (Lk 1:19).

The Archangel Gabriel was appointed by God to be the teacher of the main events connected with the Incarnation. The Incarnation was to be the espousal of the Son of God with the human nature, and God offered to Mary the choice of cooperating in it. God sent an Angel to obtain her consent in the name of humanity because it is the office of Angels to announce supernatural events to humans, and to be intermediaries between God and humankind.

God chose the Angel Gabriel. He appears to have been specially appointed to bear the messages concerning the God-Man. Gabriel fulfilled his errand with joy. It was a great honor for him to be the intermediary between Jesus and Mary, the holiest of persons, and in matters so important for the glory of God and the salvation of souls. He carried out his mission with humility and reverence in word and gesture toward the future Mother of God, whom God honored so highly.

In the greeting the Archangel Gabriel wished Mary happiness. He called her "full of grace" (Lk 1:28), describing her magnificent sharing in the work of the Incarnation by her worthy preparation for it by fullness of grace. He praised her sharing in it by union with Christ in the kind of oneness that exists between a mother and child: "The Lord is with you." He called Mary "blessed among women," above all women of the entire human race. She alone united motherhood with virginity, and therefore cooperated in the greatest of works, the redemption of mankind.

In the second part of his address Gabriel explained to Mary the object of his errand, the conception and birth of a Son Who is the Messiah. It was his privilege to reveal the holy Name of Jesus to Mary.

In the third part of his address Gabriel described how the conception of the Divine Word Incarnate was to take place, namely, by the direct action of God. This action is ascribed to the Holy Spirit because the Incarnation is the highest work of natural and supernatural perfection, the masterpiece of nature and grace, for the Savior is called the "Holy One."

Gabriel then added as a sign of the truth of his message the tidings of John's conception, and reminded Mary of the omnipotence of God.

Mary said, "I am the servant of the Lord. Let it be done to me according to your word" (Lk 1:38). With that the Angel left her. But Gabriel would be Mary's friend, teacher, and consoler.

This was the moment in which the Triune God accomplished His greatest exterior work, a work in which God created for Himself, in the Sacred Humanity of Jesus, a new kind of presence here in this world, such as had never been before; the moment in which the Father sent His Son that He might give Him to us; the moment in which the Holy Spirit, as the principle of perfection, holiness, and love, accomplished the most magnificent work of nature, grace and love; the moment in which the Second Person of the Godhead assumed our human nature and raised it to a union of life and being with Himself. At this moment began the most perfect and glorious life, overflowing with mysteries, merits and satisfaction; this life which strengthens, ennobles, and perfects all other lives.

The Archangel Gabriel was the intermediary through whom these wonders were brought to our earth. How wonderful must be his person if God chose to give him so glorious a part in the foundation of our salvation!

Saint Gabriel's role as "Strength of God" and consoler was especially evident in the life of Jesus, Mary, and Joseph. As the Angel of the Incarnation he had an important share in the mysteries of our redemption. It seems right to conclude that Gabriel the Archangel who did so much official teaching should be regarded as the angelic patron of teachers and parents who are teachers of youth. He is always ready to help them serve God in their exalted vocation.

Saint Gabriel is also a model of devotion to Jesus and Mary. He will help us to serve God with some of his faithfulness, and to love Jesus and Mary as he did.

The feast of Saints Michael, Gabriel, and Raphael is celebrated on September 29.

THE WORD OF GOD

"I am Gabriel. I stand in the presence of God and I was sent to speak to you and convey to you this good news."

—Lk 1:19

"The Angel Gabriel was sent by God to a town in Galilee called Nazareth, to a virgin betrothed to a man named Joseph, who belonged to the house of David." —Lk 1:26

"The Angel [Gabriel] said to her: 'Do not be afraid, Mary, for you have found favor with God. Behold, you will conceive in your womb and bear a Son, and you will name Him Jesus. . . . The Holy Spirit will come upon you, and the power of the Most High will overshadow you. Therefore, the Child to be born will be holy, and He will be called the Son of God.' " —Lk 1:30-35

NOVENA PRAYERS

Novena Prayer

SAINT Gabriel the Archangel, I venerate you as the "Angel of the Incarnation," because God has specially appointed you to bear the messages concerning the God-Man to Daniel, Zechariah, and the Blessed Virgin Mary. Give me a very tender and devoted love for the Incarnate Word and His blessed Mother, more like your own.

I venerate you also as the "strength from God," because you are the giver of God's strength, consoler and comforter chosen to strengthen God's faithful and to teach them important truths. I ask for the grace of a special power of the will to strive for holiness of life. Steady my resolutions, renew my courage, comfort and console me in the problems, trials, and sufferings of daily living, as you consoled our Savior in His agony and Mary in her sorrows and Joseph in his trials. I put my confidence in you.

Saint Gabriel, I ask you especially for this favor: *(Mention your request)*. Through your earnest love for the Son of God-Made-Man and for His blessed Mother, I beg of you, intercede for me that my request may be granted, if it be God's holy Will.

℣. Pray for us, Saint Gabriel the Archangel.

℟. *That we may be made worthy of the promises of Christ.*

LET us pray. Almighty and ever-living God, since You chose the Archangel Gabriel from among all the Angels to announce the mystery of Your Son's Incarnation, mercifully grant that we who honor him on earth may feel the benefit of his patronage in heaven. You live and reign forever. ℟. *Amen.*

A Prayer for Spiritual Strength

I GREET you, holy Angel Saint Gabriel, who comforted Jesus in His agony, and with you I praise the most Holy Trinity for having chosen you from among all the holy Angels to comfort and strengthen Him Who is the comfort and strength of all that are in affliction. By the honor you enjoyed and by the obedience, humility, and love with which you assisted the sacred Humanity of Jesus, my Savior, when He was fainting with sorrow at seeing the sins of the world and especially my sins, I beg of you to obtain for me perfect sorrow for my sins.

Strengthen me in the afflictions that now weigh upon my soul, and in all the other trials, to which I shall be exposed in time to come and, in particular, in my final agony. Holy Angel who strengthened Jesus Christ our Lord, come and strengthen me also.

Give me a personal and devoted love for Jesus, the Word of God Incarnate, and His Mother Mary, more like your own. May I see Them and you in heaven after my death. Amen.

Litany in Honor of Saint Gabriel
(For Private Devotion)

LORD, have mercy *Christ, have mercy.*
Lord, have mercy.
Christ, hear us.
Christ, graciously hear us.

God the Father of heaven, *have mercy on us.*
God the Son, Redeemer of the world,
God the Holy Spirit,
Holy Trinity, one God,

Jesus, King of Angels,
Mary, Queen of Angels, *pray for us.*
Saint Gabriel the Archangel,*
Strength from God,
Teacher of the nations,
Angel of the Incarnation,
Messenger of God's revelation,
Bearer of the "good news" of Redemption,
Faithful ambassador of God to Zechariah and the Virgin Mary,
Faithful Servant of the God-Man,
Angel of consolation at the Savior's agony,
Friend and consoler of the Mother of God,
Guide and helper of Saint Joseph,
Teacher and support of the prophet Daniel,
Patron of parents and teachers,
Guide to union with Jesus and Mary,
Consoler of those who suffer,
Strength of the weak,
Patron saint of modern communications,
Lamb of God, You take away the sins of the world; *spare us, O Lord.*
Lamb of God, You take away the sins of the world; *graciously hear us, O Lord.*
Lamb of God, You take away the sins of the world; *have mercy on us.*
℣. Pray for us, Saint Gabriel the Archangel.
℟. *That we may be made worthy of the promises of Christ.*

LET us pray. O God, with great wisdom You direct the ministry of Angels and human beings. Grant that those who always minister to You in heaven may defend us during our life on earth. We ask this through Christ our Lord.
℟. *Amen.*

**Pray for us* is repeated after each invocation.

38. SAINT RAPHAEL THE ARCHANGEL

(September 29)

MEDITATION

THE name of the Archangel Raphael (Hebrew: "God has healed") occurs only in the Book of Tobit of the Old Testament, where the traveling companion of the young Tobiah makes himself known as the Angel "Raphael, one of the seven Angels who stand ready to enter before the Glory of the Lord" (Tob 12:15).

It would seem that God has appointed the Angel Raphael His minister for the province of joy. The Book of Tobit shows us unhappiness followed by happiness. It tells us how Raphael appeared to the pious family of Tobit and led them by the hand away from their sadness into the peace and the glory of joy. As Tobiah, the son of Tobit, begins his journey with Raphael, his father's last prayer is that his Angel accompany him. Young Tobiah obeys his unknown guide, and because he obeys, his path is made smooth before him. The marriage of the young man offers many dangers, but the Angel Raphael is there, and sadness vanishes.

Raphael is called "the Remedy of God." Tobit had been stricken with blindness, and Sarah had been persecuted by a devil. At the same time, though many miles apart from each other, they asked God to help them. And the Scripture tells us (Tob 3:16-17): "The prayer of both these two petitioners was heard in the glorious presence of God, and Raphael was sent to heal them both."

Among the Angels, Saint Raphael is a special patron of youth. God has made this known by the beautiful Biblical account of Raphael's devotedness to the youth Tobiah. The Angel Raphael took Tobiah under his special care and protected him from the dangers that beset his journey to a strange country. He preserved Tobiah pure in a pagan world and delivered Sarah from the power of the evil spirits.

Saint Raphael is the Angel of happy meetings and a wise choice. Through him the young Tobiah was led to his future bride. Today, as in the long ago, Raphael helps people to find peace and happiness.

Raphael's devotedness to young Tobiah shows itself in the ordinary daily things of life. The young man obeys the Angel under all circumstances and in spite of his own inclinations. He is the Angel of everyday life.

Raphael is the patron of those who travel. The Church has long sanctioned the practice of praying to Saint Raphael before setting out on a trip.

If we choose Raphael as our Angel Guide and obey him as young Tobiah did, he will set the eyes of our soul on the Heavenly City toward which he is guiding us. We should walk with Raphael who directs our steadfast gaze ever toward Him Who is the Light of the world, Jesus Christ.

The feast of Saints Michael, Gabriel, and Raphael is celebrated on September 29.

THE WORD OF GOD

"I am Raphael, one of the seven Angels who stand ready to enter before the Glory of the Lord."—Tob 12:15

"When you and Sarah prayed, I was the one who presented your supplications before the Glory of the Lord."
—Tob 12:12

"Raphael . . . said to them, 'Bless God, and . . . praise Him.' "
—Tob 12:6

NOVENA PRAYERS

Novena Prayer

HOLY Archangel Raphael, standing so close to the throne of God and offering Him our prayers, I venerate you as God's special Friend and Messenger. I choose you as my Patron and wish to love and obey you as young Tobiah did. I consecrate to you my body and soul, all my work, and my whole life. I want you to be my Guide and Counselor in all the dangerous and difficult problems and decisions of my life.

Remember, dearest Saint Raphael, that the grace of God preserved you with the good

Angels in heaven when the proud ones were cast into hell. I entreat you, therefore, to help me in my struggle against the world, the spirit of impurity, and the devil. Defend me from all dangers and every occasion of sin. Direct me always in the way of peace, safety, and salvation. Offer my prayers to God as you offered those of Tobiah, so that through your intercession I may obtain the graces necessary for the salvation of my soul. I ask you to pray that God grant me this favor if it be His holy Will: *(Mention your request).*

Saint Raphael, help me to love and serve my God faithfully, to die in His grace, and finally to merit to join you in seeing and praising God forever in heaven. Amen.

Litany of Saint Raphael

(For Private Devotion)

LORD, have mercy.
Christ, have mercy.
Lord, have mercy.
Christ hear us.
Christ, graciously hear us.
God the Father of heaven,
have mercy on us.
God the Son, Redeemer of the world,
God the Holy Spirit,
Holy Trinity, one God,
Jesus, King of Angels,
Mary, Queen of Angels,
pray for us.
Saint Raphael the Archangel,*
Saint Raphael, whose name means "God has healed,"
Saint Raphael, preserved with the good Angels in God's Kingdom,
Saint Raphael, one of the seven spirits who stand before the Most High,

Pray for us is repeated after each invocation.

Saint Raphael, ministering to God in heaven,
Saint Raphael, noble and mighty Messenger of God,
Saint Raphael, devoted to the Holy Will of God,
Saint Raphael, who offered to God the prayers of the father Tobit,
Saint Raphael, traveling companion of the young Tobiah,
Saint Raphael, who guarded your friends from danger,
Saint Raphael, who found a worthy wife for Tobiah,
Saint Raphael, who delivered Sarah from the evil spirits,
Saint Raphael, who healed the father Tobit of his blindness,
Saint Raphael, guide and protector on our journey through life,
Saint Raphael, strong helper in time of need,
Saint Raphael, conqueror of evil,
Saint Raphael, guide and counselor of your people,
Saint Raphael, protector of pure souls,
Saint Raphael, patron Angel of youth,
Saint Raphael, Angel of joy,
Saint Raphael, Angel of happy meetings,
Saint Raphael, Angel of chaste courtship,
Saint Raphael, Angel of those seeking a marriage partner,
Saint Raphael, Angel of a happy marriage,
Saint Raphael, Angel of home life,
Saint Raphael, Guardian of the Christian family,
Saint Raphael, protector of travelers,
Saint Raphael, patron of health,
Saint Raphael, heavenly physician,
Saint Raphael, helper of the blind,
Saint Raphael, healer of the sick,
Saint Raphael, patron of physicians,
Saint Raphael, consoler of the afflicted,
Saint Raphael, support of the dying,

Saint Raphael, herald of blessings,

Saint Raphael, defender of the Church,

Lamb of God, You take away the sins of the world; *spare us, O Lord.*

Lamb of God, You take away the sins of the world; *graciously hear us, O Lord.*

Lamb of God, You take away the sins of the world; *have mercy on us.*

℣. Pray for us, O glorious Saint Raphael the Archangel,

℟. *That we may be made worthy of the promises of Christ.*

LET us pray. God, You graciously gave the Archangel Raphael as a companion to Your servant Tobiah on his journey. Grant us, Your servants, that we may ever enjoy his protection and be strengthened by his help. We ask this through Christ our Lord. ℟. *Amen.*

—OCTOBER—

39. SAINT THERESA OF THE CHILD JESUS

(October 1)

Patroness of the Missions

MEDITATION

THERESA was born January 2, 1873, in Alençón, France. Her parents had nine children. Of these, four died in their infancy and five entered the cloister. The father and mother were worthy examples of true Christian parents. Every morning they assisted at Holy Mass; together they received Holy Communion.

To be a spouse of Christ had been Theresa's ardent desire since the early age of three. When she was nine and again when ten years old, she begged to be received into the Carmel of Lisieux. When she completed her fifteenth year, the door of the convent finally opened to her. There the superiors put her virtues to the sharpest test. On January 10, 1889, she was invested with the holy habit and received the name Sister Theresa of the Child Jesus and of the Holy Face. She pronounced her holy vows on September 8, 1890, and gave herself to the practice of the interior life. On the path of spiritual childhood, of love and confidence, she became a great Saint.

Theresa suffered much during her short life, but it was hidden suffering, which she offered out of love for the conversion of sinners and for the sanctification of priests. She writes: "I know of one means only by which to attain perfection: Love! Let us love, since our heart is made for nothing else. I wish to give all to Jesus, since He makes me understand that He alone is perfect happiness. The good God does not need years to accomplish His work of love in a soul. Love can supply for length of years. Jesus, because He is eternal, regards not the time, but only the love."

Shortly before her death Theresa said, "I feel that my mission is about to begin, my mission of bringing others to love our good God as I love Him, and teaching souls my little way of trust and self-surrender. I will spend my heaven in doing good upon earth." Her mission was to teach souls her way of spiritual childhood. She practiced all the virtues of childhood, but those that attracted her above all were the confidence and tender love that little ones show toward their parents. Love, confidence, and self-surrender are the keys to her spiritual life.

On September 30, 1897, Theresa, a true victim of Divine Love, died of tuberculosis, a disease that in her case had assumed a very painful character. A moment before she died the patient sufferer once more made an act of perfect resignation, and with a loving glance at her crucifix, said, "Oh, I love Him! My God, I love You!" She was twenty-four years old when she died.

Saint Theresa was canonized only twenty-eight years after her death. She was declared patroness of the Foreign Missions. She was canonized by her devoted client, Pope Pius XI. The Pontiff said: "That light enkindled a love by which she lived and of which she died, having given nothing to God but love alone and having resolved to save a multitude of souls that they might love God for eternity. Her shower of mystical roses is proof that she has begun her work, and it is our most keen desire that all the faithful should study Saint Theresa so as to copy her example."

On October 19, 1997, Pope John Paul II proclaimed her the third woman Doctor of the Church. Her feast is celebrated on October 1.

THE WORD OF GOD

"Do not rejoice in the knowledge that the spirits are subject to you. Rejoice rather that your names are inscribed in heaven."

—Lk 10:20

"Unless you change and become like little children, you will never enter the Kingdom of heaven." —Mt 18:3

"Blessed are the meek, for they will inherit the earth."

—Mt 5:5

NOVENA PRAYERS

Novena Prayer

SAINT Theresa of the Child Jesus, during your short life on earth you became a mirror of angelic purity, of love strong as death, and of wholehearted abandonment to God. Now that you rejoice in the reward of your virtue, turn your eyes of mercy upon me, for I put all my confidence in you.

Obtain for me the grace to keep my heart and mind pure and clean like your own, and to abhor sincerely whatever may in any way tarnish the glorious virtue of purity, so dear to our Lord.

Most gracious Little Rose Queen, remember your promises of never letting any request made to you go unanswered, of sending down a shower of roses, and of coming down to earth to do good. Full of confidence in your power with the Sacred Heart, I implore your intercession in my behalf and beg of you to obtain the request I so ardently desire: *(Mention your request).*

Holy "Little Theresa," remember your promise "to do good upon earth" and shower down your "roses" on those who invoke you. Obtain for me from God the graces I hope for from His infinite goodness. Let me feel the power of your prayers in every need. Give me consolation in all the bitterness of this life, and especially at the hour of death, that I may be worthy to share eternal happiness with you in heaven. Amen.

Prayer

FATHER in heaven, through Saint Theresa of the Child Jesus, You desire to remind the world of the merciful love that fills Your Heart and the childlike trust we should have in You. Humbly we thank You for having crowned with such great glory Your ever-faithful child and for giving her wondrous power to bring to You, day by day, innumerable souls who will praise You eternally.

O Lord, You said, "Unless you . . . become like little children, you shall not enter the Kingdom of heaven" (Mt 18:3); grant us, we beg of You, to walk in the footsteps of Your virgin, Saint Theresa, with humility and purity of intention so that we may obtain eternal rewards. You live and reign forever. Amen.

40. THE HOLY ANGELS

(October 2)

MEDITATION

ANGELS *join us in worship.* The Angels are ministers of the infinitely good God. It is His Will that they aid us in giving Him worship. Angels preside over meetings for worship as is evident from the prayers of the Church. The Liturgy is a participation in that performed by the Angels in heaven. We should join them in giving praise to God. Their ministry consists in inspiring us with faith and love that we may worthily perform our worship. They prepare us inwardly for the reception of the Sacraments, for the Church calls on their aid.

Angels help us against evil. The Angels help us in our warfare against the evil spirit. The New Testament urges us to have faith in God, faith in Christ, and to have recourse to the weapons of God.

THE HOLY ROSARY

Prayer before the Rosary

QUEEN of the Holy Rosary, you have deigned to come to Fatima to reveal to the three shepherd children the treasures of grace hidden in the Rosary. Inspire my heart with a sincere love of this devotion, in order that by meditating on the Mysteries of our Redemption which are recalled in it, I may be enriched with its fruits and obtain peace for the world, the conversion of sinners and of Russia, and the favor which I ask of you in this Rosary. (*Here mention your request.*) I ask it for the greater glory of God, for your own honor, and for the good of souls, especially for my own. Amen.

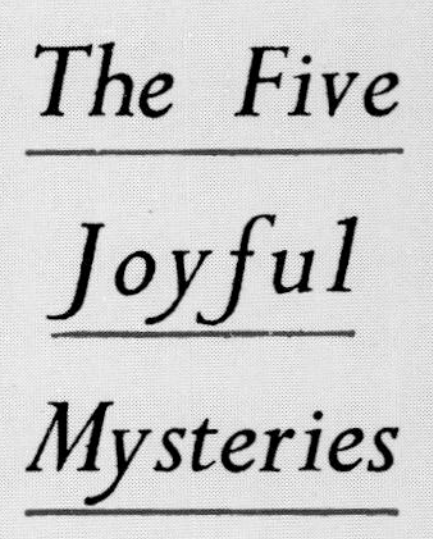

The Five Joyful Mysteries

1. The Annunciation
For the love of humility.

2. The Visitation
For charity toward my neighbor.

3. The Nativity
For the spirit of poverty.

4. The Presentation
For the virtue of obedience.

5. Finding in the Temple
For the virtue of piety.

The Five Sorrowful Mysteries

1. Agony in the Garden
For true contrition.

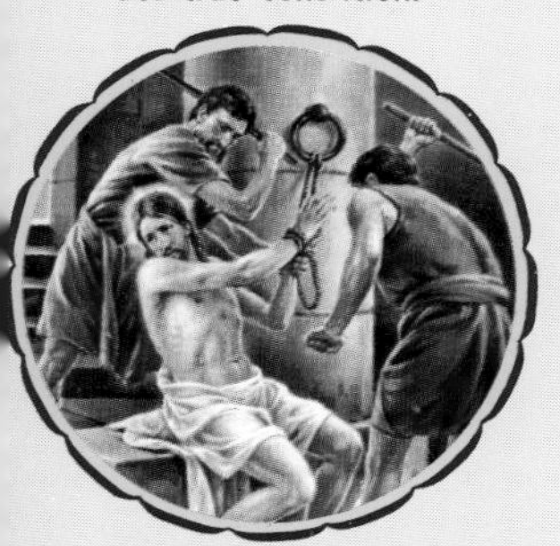

2. Scourging at the Pillar
For the virtue of purity.

3. Crowning with Thorns
For moral courage.

4. Carrying of the Cross
For the virtue of patience.

5. The Crucifixion
For final perseverance.

The Five Glorious Mysteries

1. The Resurrection
For the virtue of faith.

2. The Ascension
For the virtue of hope.

3. Descent of the Holy Spirit
For love of God.

4. Assumption of the B.V.M.
For devotion to Mary.

5. Crowning of the B.V.M.
For eternal happiness.

God sent His Angels to give us the help we need to resist evil. This is their ministry in the work of our salvation, continuing the battle once begun against Lucifer and his rebellious angels. They suggest thoughts contrary to those which the devils suggest and inspire us to turn to God in prayer. Only in heaven will we know how much they have really helped us in our warfare against evil.

The Angels long for our salvation. Since we share with the Angels in the Divine life, and since we are like them the creatures of God in Christ Jesus, they long for our salvation that we may join them in glorifying God and in enjoying the Beatific Vision.

With joy the Angels accept those God-given missions to minister to our sanctification. Victors over demons, they ask but to shield us from the enemies of our souls. We would do well to ask their assistance to repel the temptations of the evil one.

Angels also present our prayers to God by joining their own supplications to our requests. It is, therefore, to our advantage to call upon them, especially in the hour of trial and above all at the hour of death, that they may defend us from the attacks of our enemies and conduct our souls to heaven.

We have a Guardian Angel. Some among the Angels are commissioned with the care of individual souls: these are the Guardian Angels. This is the traditional doctrine of the early writers of the Church, based upon Scriptural texts and supported by solid reasons. It has been confirmed by the Church, as evidenced by the institution of a feast in honor of the Guardian Angels.

The Creator does not abandon creatures when He has made them exist; He sees that they shall have what they need for natural perfection. Christ died for all mankind and merited the means of salvation for all. Angelic assistance is part of God's universal will to save all people.

Angels also pray to God for us. In the lives of the Saints, we see an easy communication with the angelic world based on simple faith in unseen spirits whose love urges them to pray for individuals and communities before the throne of God.

While the immediate focus of the help given by the Angels is spiritual and supernatural, it includes concern for our bodily needs insofar as these pertain to salvation and sanctification.

Since our Guardian Angel keeps us in touch with heaven, we should love and venerate him and pray to him with confidence. He has ever been and is still our devoted friend, ever ready to help us on our way to heaven. In honoring our Guardian Angel we are honoring God Whom our Angel represents on this earth. We are privileged to have so beautiful and so loyal a creature of God as our friend.

THE WORD OF GOD

"I am sending an Angel before you, to keep you safe on the way and bring you to the place I have prepared. Pay attention to him and heed his voice." —Ex 23:20-21

"He has given command about you to His Angels, that they guard you in all your ways. They will bear you up upon their hands, so that you will not dash your foot against a stone." —Ps 91:11-12

"See that you do not look down upon one of these little ones. For I tell you that their Angels in heaven gaze continually on the face of My Heavenly Father." —Mt 18:10

NOVENA PRAYERS

Novena Prayer

HEAVENLY *Father,* Creator of heaven and earth, I praise and thank You, not only because You have created the visible world but also because You have created the heavens and called the numberless spirits into being. You created them most splendidly, endowing them with power and understanding, and pouring out upon them the riches of Your grace.

I praise and thank You for having showered these blessings upon the good Angels, especially upon my Guardian Angel, and for having rewarded them with eternal glory after the time of their probation. Now they surround Your throne forever, singing jubilantly: Holy, holy, holy, Lord God of hosts! Heaven and earth are full of Your glory. Hosanna in the highest!

Eternal Son of God, I honor You as the King of the Angels. Yet You Yourself were pleased to take their name and office and to dwell among us as the Angel and Messenger of God. You were the faithful Companion and constant Leader of the chosen people. By Your Incarnation You became the Ambassador of our heavenly Father and the Messenger of the great decree of our redemption.

For Your greater glory, loving King of the Angels, I wish to praise and honor Your servants, the Holy Angels, especially my own Guardian Angel. In union with these Holy

Angels I adore and revere You as my Savior and my God.

Holy Spirit, Divine Artist, Finger of God's right hand, by Your power and love the hosts of the Angels were brought into being to adore and serve God. They do so with constant fidelity and ready obedience. They carry out Your commands with fervent love and holy zeal. Divine Spirit, You also created us in Your likeness and made of our souls Your living temples.

I thank You for having given us Your Holy Angels to help, protect, and guide us that we may persevere in Your grace throughout life's journey and safely reach our heavenly home. Help me to be attentive to their guidance that I may do Your holy Will perfectly and at the same time find true happiness in this life and in the next.

Most Holy Trinity, Father, Son, and Holy Spirit, in honor of the Holy Angels, I ask You to grant my special request if it be Your holy Will: *(Mention your request).*

Prayer to the Angels

ANGELS and Archangels, Thrones and Dominations, Principalities and Powers, Virtues of the heavens, Cherubim and Seraphim, praise the Lord forever.

Praise the Lord, all you His Angels, who are mighty in strength and who carry out His commands. Praise the Lord, all you His hosts, His servants who do His Will.

Holy Angel who strengthened Jesus Christ our Lord, come and strengthen us also. Come and do not delay!

Prayer to Our Guardian Angel

MY dear Guardian Angel, you were given to me by my merciful God to be the faithful companion of my earthly exile. I honor and love you as my most devoted friend to whom God has entrusted the care of my immortal soul. With all my heart I thank you for your love and constant care of me.

Dearest Angel-friend, I beg you to guard and protect me, a poor sinner. Conduct me on the way of life. Warn me against every occasion of sin, and fill my soul with wholesome thoughts and loving encouragement to practice virtue. Intercede for me that I may share in your burning zeal in God's service and devoted love for His Divine Will.

Forgive me, loving Guardian, for so often disregarding your advice in the past and for ignoring your inspirations. I shall try in the future to obey you willingly and faithfully. You know the value of my soul in the eyes of God. Never permit me to forget that it was redeemed by the Precious Blood of Jesus Christ. Let no stain of evil disfigure the beauty of my soul, nor any sinful thought or deed rob me of my dignity as a child of God. Keep me from scandal that I may never become an occasion of sin to others and thus destroy the work that Christ has wrought in their souls by His bitter Passion and Death.

Dear Guardian Angel, may I enjoy your protection in this dangerous journey through life that I may reach my eternal home in heaven, there to praise the mercy of God toward me in union with you and all the other Angels and Saints forever. Amen.

Prayer

GOD, in Your Providence You were pleased to send Your Holy Angels to keep watch over us. Grant that we may always be defended and shielded by them and rejoice in their companionship.

Lord, we pray You to visit our home and drive far from it all snares of the enemy. Let Your Holy Angels dwell in it to preserve us in peace. Let Your blessing be always upon us.

Almighty and Everlasting God, in Your loving Providence, You have appointed for all the faithful from their birth a special Angel to be Guardian of their body and soul. Grant that I may so love and honor him whom You have given me, that, protected by Your grace and his help, I may merit to behold, with him and all the angelic host, the glory of Your face in the heavenly Kingdom. You live and reign forever. Amen.

41. SAINT JUDE THADDEUS

Apostle of Those in Need

(October 28)

MEDITATION

SAINT Jude Thaddeus was closely associated with our Lord by blood relationship through Saints Joachim and Anne, the parents of the Blessed Virgin. A grand-nephew of these two saints, he is at once a nephew of Mary and Joseph, which places him in the relationship of cousin of our Lord.

Jude is the brother of the Apostle James the Less. He had two other brothers, whom the Gospel calls "brethren" of Jesus. When our Lord came back from Judea to Nazareth, he began to teach in the synagogue. The people who heard Him were astonished and said, "Where did this man get this wisdom and these miraculous powers? Isn't this the carpenter's

Son? Isn't Mary known to be His mother and aren't James, Joseph, Simon, and [Jude] His brothers?" (Mt 13:54).

The word "brethren" or "brothers" in the Hebrew language usually suggests a near relationship. Jude's father was Clopas. His mother's name was Mary. She was a near relative of the Blessed Virgin. She stood beneath the Cross when Jesus died. "Standing near the Cross of Jesus were His Mother, His Mother's sister, Mary the wife of Clopas, and Mary Magdalene" (Jn 19:25).

In his boyhood and youth Jude must have associated with Jesus. At the beginning of the public life of Jesus, Jude left all to follow the Master. As an Apostle, he labored with great zeal for the conversion of the Gentiles. For ten years he worked as a missionary in the whole of Mesopotamia. He returned to Jerusalem for the Council of the Apostles. Later he joined Simon in Libya, where the two Apostles preached the Gospel to the barbarian inhabitants.

Tradition says that he and Simon suffered martyrdom at Suanis, a city of Persia, where they had labored as missionaries. Jude was beaten to death with a club; hence he is represented with a club in his hand. His head was then severed from his body with an ax. His body was brought to Rome and his relics are now venerated in Saint Peter's Basilica.

Saint Jude is known mainly as the author of the New Testament Epistle of Jude. This letter was probably written before the fall of Jerusalem, between the years 62 and 65. In his letter Jude denounces the heresies of that early time and warns the Christians against the seduction of false teaching. He speaks of the judgment to come upon the heretics who are living evil lives and condemns the worldly-minded, the lustful, and "those who cultivate people for the sake of gain." He encourages Christians to remain steadfast in the faith and foretells that false teachers, leading wicked lives and ridiculing religion, will arise, but that they will be punished.

To the pride of the wicked he opposes the humble loyalty of the Archangel Michael. He encourages the Christians to build a spiritual edifice by living lives founded upon faith, love of God, hope, and prayer. He encourages the practice of love of neighbor; he urges Christians to endeavor to convert the heretics by the virtues of their lives.

Jude concludes the letter with a prayer praising God for the Incarnation, by means of which the eternal Word of God, Jesus Christ, took upon Himself our human nature and redeemed mankind.

The feast of Saints Simon and Jude is celebrated on October 28.

THE WORD OF GOD

"Amen, amen, I say to you, whoever has faith in Me will do the works I do, and far greater than these."

—Jn 14:12

"Isn't this the carpenter's Son? Isn't Mary known to be His Mother and aren't James, Joseph, Simon, and [Jude] His brothers?"

—Mt 13:54

"Build yourselves up in your most holy faith and pray in the Holy Spirit. Persevere in God's love and wait for the mercy of our Lord Jesus Christ that leads to eternal life."

—Jude 20-21

NOVENA PRAYERS

Novena Prayer

GLORIOUS Saint Jude Thaddeus, by those sublime privileges with which you were adorned in your lifetime, namely, your relationship with our Lord Jesus Christ according to the flesh, and your vocation to be an Apostle, and by that glory which now is yours in heaven as the reward of your apostolic labors and your martyrdom, obtain for me from the Giver of every good and perfect gift all the graces of which I stand in need: *(Mention your request).*

May I treasure up in my heart the divinely inspired doctrines that you have given us in your Epistle: to build my edifice of holiness upon our most holy faith, by praying for the grace of the Holy Spirit; to keep myself in the love of God, looking for the mercy of Jesus Christ unto eternal life; to strive by all means to help those who go astray.

May I thus praise the glory and majesty, the dominion and power of Him Who is able to keep me without sin and to present me spotless with great joy at the coming of our Divine Savior, the Lord Jesus Christ. Amen.

Consecration to Saint Jude

SAINT Jude, Apostle of Christ and glorious martyr, I desire to honor you with a special devotion. I choose you as my patron and protector. To you I entrust my soul and my body, all my spiritual and temporal interests, as well as those of my family. To you I consecrate my mind so that in all things it may be enlightened by faith; my heart so that you may keep it pure and fill it with love for Jesus and Mary; my will so that, like yours, it may always be one with the Will of God.

I beg you to help me to master my evil inclinations and temptations and to avoid all occasions of sin. Obtain for me the grace of never offending God, of fulfilling faithfully all the duties of my state of life, and of practicing all those virtues that are needful for my salvation.

Pray for me, my holy patron and helper, so that, being inspired by your example and assisted by your prayers, I may live a holy life, die a happy death, and attain to the glory of heaven, there to love and thank God forever. Amen.

Prayer

O GOD, You made Your Name known to us through the Apostles. By the intercession of Saint Jude, let Your Church continue to grow with an increased number of believers. Grant this through Christ our Lord. Amen.

—NOVEMBER—

42. OUR PATRON SAINT

(All Saints, November 1)

MEDITATION

SAINTS are those who distinguish themselves by heroic virtue during life and whom the Church honors as Saints either by her ordinary universal teaching authority or by a solemn definition called canonization. The Church's official recognition of sanctity implies that the persons are now in heavenly glory, that they may be publicly invoked everywhere and that their virtues during life or Martyr's death is a witness and example to the Christian faithful.

The Church honors the Saints who are already with the Lord in heaven because they inspire us by the heroic example of their lives and intercede for us with God.

Because of our union with Christ we are united with all those who share His life in the larger family of God, the Communion of Saints. We on earth, members of the Church Militant, still fighting the good fight as soldiers of Christ, still journeying on our way to our Father's house, are helped by the prayers and encouragement of the victorious and blessed members of the family, the Church Triumphant in heaven. We honor the Saints and endeavor to imitate the example of their virtuous lives.

We manifest the love and unity that are ours in the Communion of Saints also by praying to the Saints in heaven as our patrons and intercessors with God. Not only is their intercession with God very powerful because of the love they have shown Him on earth, but we also share in their merits gained by their heroic life.

A Patron Saint or Blessed is one who, since early Christian times, has been chosen as a special intercessor with God for a particular person, place, community, or organization. The custom arose from the Biblical fact that a change of personal name indicated a change in the person, e.g., Abram to Abraham, Simon to Peter, Saul to Paul; and from the practice of having churches built over the tombs of Martyrs.

At Baptism and Confirmation we have received the name of a Saint whom we should imitate and whose intercession we should invoke. We should frequently pray to our Patron Saint for the needs of soul and body, especially on the Saint's feast day. We can honor our Patron Saint by making a novena in his or her honor.

THE WORD OF GOD

"[O Lord,] with Your Blood You have purchased persons for God from every tribe and language, people and nation. You made them into a Kingdom and priests to serve our God, and they will reign on the earth."

—Rev 5:9-10

"We are the temple of the living God, just as God has said: I will live in them and walk among them. I will be their God, and they will be My people." —2 Cor 6:16

"Just as the One Who called you is holy, be holy yourselves in all you do; for it is written, 'Be holy, because I am holy.' " —1 Pet 1:15-16

NOVENA PRAYERS

Novena Prayer

GREAT Saint N., at my Baptism you were chosen as a guardian and witness of my obligations, and under your name I then became an adopted child of God, and solemnly renounced Satan, his works, and his empty promises. Assist me by your powerful intercession in the fulfillment of these sacred promises. You also made them in the days of your earthly pilgrimage, and your fidelity in keeping them to the end has obtained for you an everlasting reward in heaven.

I am called to the same happiness that you enjoy. The same help is offered to me that enabled you to acquire eternal glory. You overcame temptations like those that I experience.

Pray for me, therefore, my Holy Patron, so that, being inspired by your example and assisted by your prayers, I may live a holy life, die a happy death, and reach eternal life to praise and thank God in heaven with you.

I ask you to pray to God for this special request if it be God's holy Will: *(Mention your request).*

Prayer

ALMIGHTY, eternal God, You were pleased to make Your Church illustrious through the varied splendor of the Saints. As we venerate their memory may we also follow such shining examples of virtue on earth and thus obtain merited crowns in heaven. We ask this through Christ our Lord. Amen.

"Eternal rest grant to them, O Lord, and let perpetual light shine upon them. May they rest in peace. Amen."

Part Four

THE HOLY SOULS IN PURGATORY

43. FOR THE POOR SOULS IN PURGATORY

(November 2)

MEDITATION

GOD created human beings that they might possess their Creator in the Beatific Vision. But nothing defiled can enter heaven, and therefore those who are less than perfect must first be purified before they can be admitted to the vision of God. The Church teaches that there exists purgatory, in which the souls of the just who die with the stains of sins are cleansed by expiation before they are admitted to heaven. They can be helped, however, by the prayers of the faithful on earth.

The souls of the just are those that leave the body in the state of sanctifying grace and are therefore destined by right to enter heavenly glory. Their particular judgment was favorable, but they must first be cleansed before they can see the face of God.

"The stains of sins" means the temporal punishment due to mortal or venial sins already forgiven as to guilt but not fully remitted as to penalty when a person dies. It may also mean the venial sins themselves, not forgiven as to either guilt or punishment before death. The Church understands purgatory to mean the state or condition under which the faithful departed undergo purification.

The teaching of the Church about purgatory finds corroboration in the Bible. The text of 2 Maccabees 12:46 presupposes after-death purification. So do the words of our Lord: "Whoever speaks against the Holy Spirit will not be forgiven, either in this world or in the world to come" (Mt 12:32). A similar conclusion can be drawn from 1 Corinthians 3:11-15.

The Catholic practice of praying for the poor souls is based on the Church's faith in the Communion of Saints. The members of the Mystical Body can help each other, whether still on earth or already in the life beyond the grave. A study of the Church's liturgical prayers reveals that Saints and Angels are often invoked for the Church Suffering, but always to intercede. Anyone in the state of grace can pray effectively for the poor souls; at least the state of grace is probably necessary to gain indulgences for the deceased.

The Second Vatican Council made a profession of belief in the Church Suffering, saying it "accepts with great devotion this venerable faith of our ancestors regarding this vital fellowship with our brothers and sisters who are in heavenly glory or who, having died, are still being purified."

Although not defined doctrine, it is commonly held that the essential pain in purgatory is the pain of loss, because the souls are temporarily deprived of the beatific vision. However, there is no comparison between this suffering and the pains of hell. It is temporary and therefore includes the assured hope of one day seeing the face of God. It is borne with patience, since the souls realize that purification is necessary. It is accepted generously, out of love for God and with perfect submission to His will.

Probably the pains in purgatory are gradually diminished, so that in the latter stages we could not compare sufferings on earth with the state of a soul approaching the vision of God. But the souls also experience intense spiritual joy. The souls are absolutely sure of their salvation. They have faith, hope, and great charity. They know themselves to be in Divine friendship, confirmed in grace, and no longer able to offend God.

Although the souls in purgatory cannot merit, they are able to pray and obtain the fruit of prayer. The power of their prayers depends on their sanctity. It is certain that they can pray and obtain blessings for those living on earth. They are united with the pilgrim Church in the Communion of Saints. We are therefore encouraged to invoke their aid, with the confidence of being heard by those who understand our needs so well from their own experience and who are grateful for the prayers and sacrifices and Holy Masses we offer on their behalf.

THE WORD OF GOD

"[Judas Maccabee] took up a collection . . . to provide for an expiatory sacrifice . . . focusing on the splendid reward reserved for those whose death was marked by godliness. Therefore, he had this expiatory sacrifice offered for the dead so that they might be delivered from their sin." —2 Mac 12:43-46

"Whoever speaks a word against the Son of Man will be forgiven, but whoever speaks against the Holy Spirit will not be forgiven, either in this world or in the world to come." —Mt 12:32

"If anyone builds on that foundation [of Christ] with gold, silver, and precious stones, or with wood, hay, and straw, the work of each person will come to light. For the Day will disclose it, because it will be revealed with fire, and the fire itself will test the worth of each person's work. If what has been built on the foundation survives, the builder will be rewarded. If it burns down, the builder will suffer loss. The builder will be saved, though only by passing through fire." —1 Cor 3:12-15

NOVENA PRAYERS

Novena Prayer

MERCIFUL *Father*, in union with the Church Triumphant in heaven, I beg of You, have mercy on the souls in purgatory. Be mindful of Your eternal love for them and show them Your mercy because of the boundless merits of Your beloved Son. Be pleased to free them from pain and sorrow that they may soon enjoy eternal peace and happiness. God, Heavenly Father, I thank You for the grace of perseverance which you have granted to the souls of the faithful departed.

Loving Savior, *Jesus Christ*, You are the King of kings in the land of eternal bliss. I beg of You, in Your mercy hear my prayer and set free the holy souls in purgatory, especially N. . . . Lead them from the prison of darkness to the light and freedom of the children of God in the Kingdom of Your glory. Loving Savior, I thank You for having redeemed the poor souls with Your most Precious Blood and saved them from eternal death.

God *Holy Spirit,* enkindle in me the fire of Your Divine love. Arouse my faith and confidence, and graciously accept the prayers I offer You for the suffering souls in purgatory.

I wish to apply the merits of this devotion to the entire Church Suffering, but especially to my deceased parents, brothers, sisters, benefactors, relatives, and friends. Hear my prayer that we may be united with them in the Kingdom of Your glory.

God *Holy Spirit,* I thank You for all the graces with which You have sanctified, strengthened, and comforted these holy souls, and especially for consoling them in their present sufferings with the certainty of eternal bliss. May they soon be united with You and hear those blessed words that will call them to their heavenly home: "Come, you who are blessed by My Father, inherit the Kingdom prepared for you from the foundation of the world" (Mt 25:34).

For Deceased Parents

GOD, You commanded us to honor our father and our mother. In Your mercy have pity on the soul of my father (mother), and forgive him (her) his (her) sins. May I see him (her) again in the joy of everlasting brightness. Grant this through Christ our Lord. Amen.

For Our Family

GOOD Jesus, Your loving Heart was ever moved by the sorrows of others. Look with pity on the souls of my dear ones in purgatory. Hear my cry for mercy, and grant that those whom You called from our home and hearts may soon enjoy everlasting rest in the home of Your love in heaven.

Prayer

GOD, our Creator and Redeemer, by Your power Christ conquered death and returned to You in glory. May all Your people who have gone before us in faith (especially N. . . .) share His victory and enjoy the vision of Your glory forever, where Christ lives and reigns with You and the Holy Spirit, one God, forever. Amen.

Eternal rest grant to them, O Lord, and let perpetual light shine upon them. May they rest in peace. Amen.

Merciful Lord Jesus, grant them everlasting rest.

Mary, Mother of God and Mother of mercy, pray for us and for all who have died in the embrace of the Lord. Amen.

"Ask, and it will be given you; seek, and you will find; knock, and the door will be opened to you" (Lk 11:9).

Part Five

PERSONAL NEEDS

44. NOVENA FOR HEALTH

MEDITATION

NOTHING in nature happens by chance. All creatures have a reason for their existence. There is also a reason for the existence of pain in the world, otherwise God would never permit it.

It is not for us to question God's Divine plan. Our duty is to accept life with its sorrows and joys willingly. As creatures we are bound to God, our Creator. He did not abandon us after bringing us into this life, and He does not intend to do so. We must pray for faith that we may be able to fit the stark realities of life into His Divine plan. Our daily trials cannot harm us unless we rebel against them and God's plan.

Suffering, sadness and cares come to us to remind us that earth is not a paradise and that the life, truth, and love we crave are not to be found here below. The possession of God is our end in life, as Saint Augustine wrote: "You have made us for Yourself, Lord, and our hearts are restless until they rest in You."

Jesus is our model of suffering willingly. Bodily suffering, mental anguish, bitter disappointment, the false judgment of justice, the betrayal of true friendship, the court's perversion of honesty, and the violent separation from a mother's love—all these Jesus took upon Himself knowingly, freely, and willingly. Then after the crucifixion, He uttered a word of triumph, "It is finished" (Jn 19:30).

It was all according to His Father's plan. On the Cross the plan was finished. Its full meaning was not revealed until three days later, when the Seed that fell to the ground arose into the newness of Life. It was this plan Jesus gave to the disciples on the way to Emmaus, "Was it not necessary that the Messiah should suffer these things and enter into His glory?" (Lk 24:26).

Suffering, then, has a part in our Father's plan. Sickness can be the cause of much suffering, but Jesus said, "Come to Me, all you who are weary and overburdened, and I will give you rest. Take My yoke upon you and learn from Me, for I am meek and humble of heart, and you will find rest for your souls. For My yoke is easy and My burden light" (Mt 11:28-30). "Amen, amen, I say to you, if you ask the Father anything in My Name, He will give it to you" (Jn 16:23).

It is God's Will that you pray and in this way His promise will be fulfilled, "Ask, and it will be given you; seek, and you will find; knock, and the door will be opened to you" (Lk 11:9). Therefore, it is right to pray for good health.

THE WORD OF GOD

"You will weep and mourn while the world rejoices. You will be sorrowful, but your grief will turn into joy . . . and no one shall deprive you of your joy." —Jn 16:20-22

"Insofar as you are sharing in the sufferings of Christ, you should rejoice, so that your joy will be without limit when His glory is revealed." —1 Pet 4:13

"God is faithful, and He will not allow you to be tried beyond your strength. But along with the trial He will also provide a way out and the strength to bear it."
—1 Cor 10:13

"Ask, and it will be given you; seek, and you will find; knock, and the door will be opened to you." —Lk 11:9

NOVENA PRAYERS

Novena Prayer

JESUS, Divine Physician, You have created nature and all the wondrous functions of the human body. You are the Master of Your creation. You can and do suspend the laws of nature for those who have faith in Your goodness and entreat You in fervent prayer. You said, "Ask, and it will be given you; seek, and you will find; knock, and the door will be opened to you" (Lk 11:9). Full of confidence in this promise, I beg You to help me in my present need: *(Mention your request).*

Jesus, during Your lifetime You cured sickness and disease and even raised the dead to life, because people asked You to do so in prayer. I firmly believe that You will hear my prayer also, if this should be the Will of God.

I ask for the grace to understand more and more the infinite love of Your Sacred Heart for me. I firmly believe that You love me with a love that ordains all things for my own good even though this may be difficult for my nature to bear. It is a love that turns to good all that I may at the moment consider evil. I love Your Heart that loves me so much.

Jesus, my Savior, I thank You for being my best Friend in any illness of my life and my Companion in suffering: I thank You for loving me with a Heart human like my own—a Heart that can understand my sorrows and problems since It has experienced all that I must bear; a Heart that can sympathize with me and befriend me in my hour of need; a Heart that can love me with the love of the best of friends. Your Heart burns for me with a love that knows no end because It has its source in the depths of the Godhead. Not all the affection You pour out upon countless other souls lessens Your love for me.

Jesus, I unite myself with You as You offer yourself during the Holy Sacrifice of the Mass and renew Your Sacrifice of Calvary. Give my heart sentiments like Your own, so that through frequent Holy Communion and prayer I may become holy and pleasing to God, a worthy sacrifice with You. May all the actions, sufferings, tears, and disappointments of my life be thus consecrated to You as a sacrifice for the glory of God.

Give me the grace to bear cheerfully and willingly everything that You send me, or permit in my life, whether favorable or unfavorable, for I am resolved to conform myself to the Divine Will in all things. May God's Will always be my will! Amen.

Prayer to Our Lady, Health of the Sick

MY dearest Mother Mary, I confidently invoke you as the Health of the Sick. You are the loving Mother especially of those who are blessed with a cross, particularly illness. I humbly plead for this favor: *(Mention your request).*

Mother of Perpetual Help, I beg you to present my petition to your Divine Son. If you will pray for me, I cannot be refused, for your prayers before God are powerful. With child-like trust I abandon myself to God's holy Will concerning my request.

Mother of Mercy, I love you; I put all my confidence in you. I offer to God through your hands every suffering that I must bear, with all the love of my heart. Make every pain an act of love for God, an act of atonement for my sins, and meritorious for the salvation of souls, especially for my own soul. Teach me patience and resignation to the holy Will of God, in imitation of you, dear Mother of Sorrows.

℣. Pray for us, Our Lady, Health of the Sick.

℟. *That we may be made worthy of the promises of Christ.*

LET us pray. Grant us, Your servants, we beg You, Lord God, that we may be blessed with health of soul and body, and by the glorious intercession of the Blessed Virgin Mary, Health of the Sick, be freed from the sorrows of this present life and enjoy everlasting bliss. We ask this through Christ our Lord. Amen.

Prayer for Patience in Sickness

HEAVENLY Father, Your Son accepted our sufferings to teach us the virtue of patience in human illness. Hear my prayer and help me in my sufferings. May I realize that You have chosen me to be a Saint through my sufferings and that I am joined to Christ in His suffering for the salvation of the world.

Show me the power of Your loving care and restore my health, if it be Your Will, that I may offer joyful thanks in Your Church.

Direct my heart and body in the love of You and the patience of Christ. Help me, defend me from all evil and bring me safely to life everlasting.

Heavenly Father, Your will be done!

45. NOVENA FOR OUR FAMILY

MEDITATION

THE calling of every family is to share life together with a deep, personal love according to God's Will. It is the family's calling to become a community, sharing life together in deep love and respect for each other. The family is the most sacred of all societies. Our character, beliefs, thoughts, and virtues come from good loving parents.

Family life has this aim: that the spouses be ready with generous hearts to work together with the love of the Creator Who through them will enlarge and enrich His own family day by day.

Marriage is a lifelong partnership of love. The giving of self in marriage brings children who make the love of husbands and wives richer and fulfills one of the purposes of marriage. If husbands and wives are generous to God in working with Him according to His Will, enlarging His own family on earth, He will bless them in this life and especially in heaven.

This blessing of God can be expressed in the form of the Eight Beatitudes, given to us by Jesus in His Sermon on the Mount. There are Eight Beatitudes for the Home.

1. Blessed is the home where the father, mother, and children love God sincerely and keep His commandments faithfully, go to Confession regularly, receive Holy Communion frequently, and pray much; for the Lord lives in such a home.

2. Blessed is the home in which the Sundays and holy days are properly observed, for the members will one day meet again at the festival of heaven.

3. Blessed is the home which no one leaves to go to sinful amusements, for in it the joy of Christ shall reign.

4. Blessed is the home where unkind speech does not enter, nor cursing, nor bad literature, nor intemperance, for on that home will be heaped the blessings of peace.

5. Blessed is the home where father and mother are conscious of the sacred dignity of bringing children into the world and educating them in the service of God, where they faithfully fulfill the obligations they have toward each other and their children, and detest the sins sometimes committed in the married state, for they will merit the favor and abundant blessings of God.

6. Blessed is the home to which a priest is called in time and often to attend the sick, for their illness will have its consolation and death will be happy.

7. Blessed is the home where Christian doctrine is properly appreciated and learned from the catechism and good books, for in that home the faith will be kept firm and active.

8. Blessed is the home where the parents find their joy in children who are dutiful and obedient, and where the children find in their parents the example of the fear and love of God, for that home will be the home of just people, the haven of virtues, and the ark of salvation.

We must pray earnestly and often that these blessings of God come upon our family. We can do so by making an occasional novena for our family. No one deserves this more than the persons we love so dearly in our family.

THE WORD OF GOD

"Honor your father and your mother so that you may enjoy a long life in the land that the Lord, your God, has given you." —Ex 20:12

"Let your father and your mother exult; let the one who brought you forth rejoice." —Prov 23:24

"Happy are those who fear the Lord and walk in His ways. . . . Within your house your wife will be like a fruitful vine; around your table your children will be like shoots of an olive tree." —Ps 128:1-3

NOVENA PRAYERS

Novena Prayer

GOD of goodness and mercy, to Your fatherly protection we commend our family, our household and all that belongs to us. We entrust all to Your love and keeping. Fill our home with Your blessings as You filled the holy House of Nazareth with Your presence.

Above all things else, keep far from us the stain of sin. We want You alone to reign over us. Help each one of us to obey Your holy laws, love You sincerely, and imitate Your example, the example of Mary, Jesus' Mother and ours, and the example of the holy guardian Saint Joseph.

Lord, preserve us and our home from all evils and misfortunes, but grant that we may be ever resigned to Your Divine Will even in the sorrows which it may please You to send, or in any cross you may permit to come to us.

Give all of us the grace to live in perfect harmony and charity toward our neighbor. Grant that every one of us may deserve by a holy life the comfort of Your holy Sacraments at the hour of death.

We also ask You to grant us this special request: *(Mention your request).*

Bless our home, God the Father, Who created us, God the Son, Who suffered for us upon the Cross, and God the Holy Spirit, Who sanctified us in Baptism. One God in Three Divine Persons, preserve our bodies, purify our minds, direct our hearts, and bring us all to everlasting life!

Consecration to the Sacred Heart of Jesus

MOST Sacred Heart of Jesus, You revealed to Saint Margaret Mary Your desire to rule over Christian families. Behold, in order to please You, we consecrate our family to Your Sacred Heart and proclaim Your Reign over us.

We want to live Your life. May the Virtues to which You have promised peace on earth flower in our family. Keep far from us the spirit of the world which You have condemned.

Jesus, be the King of our minds by the simplicity of our faith. Be the King of our hearts by our love of You alone; help us to keep alive this flame of love in our hearts by receiving Holy Communion frequently and by prayer.

Sacred Heart of Jesus, be pleased to preside over us when we assemble. Bless our spiritual and temporal affairs, ward off all trouble, sanctify our joys, and give us consolation in sorrows.

If any of us should have the misfortune of offending You, Heart of Jesus, give that person the grace to remember that You are kind and merciful to the repentant sinner.

When the hour of separation strikes and death enters our family circle, whether we go or whether we stay, help us all to submit humbly to Your eternal decrees. Let it be our consolation to remember that the day will come when our entire family, once more united in heaven, will praise Your glory and goodness forever.

May the Immaculate Heart of Mary and the glorious Patriarch Saint Joseph be pleased to offer You this our act of consecration.

Consecration to the Holy Family

JESUS, our most loving Redeemer, You came to enlighten the world with Your teaching and example. You willed to spend the greater part of Your life in humble obedience to Mary and Joseph in the poor home of Nazareth. In this way You sanctified that Family which was to be an example for all Christian families.

Graciously accept our family which we dedicate and consecrate to You. Be pleased to protect, guard, and keep it in holy fear, in peace, and in the harmony of Christian charity. By conforming ourselves to the Divine model of your Family, may we all attain to eternal happiness.

Mary, Mother of Jesus and our Mother, by your merciful intercession make this our humble offering acceptable to Jesus, and obtain for us graces and blessings.

Saint Joseph, most holy guardian of Jesus and Mary, help us by your prayers in all our spiritual and temporal needs so that we may praise Jesus our Divine Savior, together with Mary and you, for all eternity.

Prayer

LORD, we pray that You visit our home and drive far from it all snares of the enemy. Let Your Holy Angels dwell in it to preserve us in peace; and let Your blessing be always upon us.

Through the prayers of the Blessed Virgin Mary, we beg You to guard our family from all danger. And as we humbly worship You with all our hearts, in Your mercy graciously protect us from all the snares of the enemy and keep us in Your peace. We ask this through Jesus Christ our Lord. Amen.

Petition to Jesus, Mary, and Joseph

DEAR Jesus, Mary, and Joseph, to you we consecrate our family and all that we have. We want our home to belong entirely to you. You made family life holy by your family life at Nazareth. Your home was a home of prayer, love, patient endurance, and toil.

It is our earnest wish to model our home upon yours at Nazareth. Remain with us, so that with your help the purity of our morals may be preserved, that we may obey the Commandments of God and of the Church, and receive the Sacraments frequently.

Willingly we surrender our entire freedom to you, our Queen and our Mother. We place under your care our body and its senses, our soul and its faculties, our thoughts and desires, our words and deeds, our joys and sorrows, our life and our death.

Give your aid to our family, to our relatives, and to all who do us good. Under your guidance may we always follow the Holy Spirit and never hinder His grace in us through sin.

Help us to tread our way successfully through the dangers of this life and so win passage to our home country in heaven. As Saints there with you, may we sing the praises of each Person of the Blessed Trinity for all eternity.

Keep love and peace in our midst. Console us in our troubles. Help us to preserve the innocence of our children. Enlighten and strengthen our growing sons and daughters. Assist us all at the hour of death, so that we may be united with each other and with you in heaven.

Prayer to the Heavenly Father

FATHER, our family looks to Your loving guidance and order as the pattern of all family life. By following the example of the Holy Family of Your Son, in mutual love and respect, may we come to the joy of our home in heaven.

Father, by the power of Your Spirit You have filled the hearts of Your faithful people with gifts of love for one another. Hear the prayers I offer for our family, relatives, and benefactors. Give us health of mind and body that we may do Your Will with perfect love.

Pardon our sins. Give us Your constant encouragement and guide us throughout our lives, until the day when we, with all who have served You, will rejoice in Your presence forever in heaven. Amen.

"Let your main focus be on [God's] Kingdom and His righteousness, and all these things will be given you as well" (Mt 6:33).

Part Six

SPIRITUAL NEEDS

PRAYERS OF PETITION FOR HOLINESS OF LIFE

To Love God Above All

GOD, my Father,
may I love You in all things
and above all things. May I reach the joy
You have prepared for me in heaven.
Nothing is good that is against Your Will,
and all is good that comes from Your hand.
Place in my heart a desire to please You
and fill my mind with thoughts of Your love,
so that I may grow in Your wisdom
and enjoy Your peace.

To Become More Like Jesus

GOD, our Father, You redeemed us
and made us Your children in Christ.
Through Him You have saved us from death
and given us Your Divine life of grace.
By becoming more like Jesus on earth,
may I come to share His glory in heaven.
Give me the peace of Your kingdom,
which this world does not give.
By Your loving care
protect the good You have given me.
Open my eyes to the wonders of Your love
that I may serve You with a willing heart.

The Way to Peace

FATHER of love, hear my prayer.
Help me to know Your Will
and to do it with courage and faith.
Accept my offering of myself—
all my thoughts, words, deeds and sufferings.
May my life be spent giving You glory.
Give me the strength to follow Your call,
so that Your truth may live in my heart
and bring peace to me and to those I meet
for I believe in Your love.

To Know the Way to Peace

FATHER of heaven and earth, hear my prayer,
and show me the way to peace.
Guide each effort of my life,
so that my faults and my sins
may not keep me from the peace You promised.
May the new life of grace You give me
through the Eucharist and prayer
make my love for You grow
and keep me in the joy of Your Kingdom.

To Follow Mary's Example

LORD Jesus Christ,
help me to follow the example of Mary,
always ready to do Your will.
At the message of an Angel
she welcomed You, God's Son,
and, filled with the light of Your Spirit,
she became Your temple.

Through her prayers for me
take away my weakness
and make the offering of my life with You
in the Holy Sacrifice of the Mass
pleasing to You and to the Father.
May I rejoice in the gift of Your grace
and be united with You and Mary in glory.

For Faith, Hope, Love

LORD my God,
help me to love You with all my heart
and to love all people as You love them.
May I serve You with my every desire
and show love for others even as You love me.
May my faith continue to grow.
Give me the grace I need for my salvation.
Watch over me,
for all my hope is in You.
Through Your mercy and loving kindness,
through the offering of Jesus in the Mass,
and the prayers of His loving Mother,
grant me Your blessings to lead me
to the treasures of Your heavenly Kingdom.

To Live in God's Presence

GOD, my Father,
You have promised to remain forever
with those who do what is just and right.
Help me to live in Your presence.
The loving plan of Your wisdom
was made known when Jesus, Your Son,
became man like one of us.

I want to obey His commandment of love
and bring Your peace and joy to others.
Keep before me the wisdom and love
You have made known in Your Son.
Help me to be like Him in word and deed.

To Share the Life of Jesus

LOVING Father,
faith in Your word is the way to wisdom.
Help me to think about Your Divine plan
that I may grow in the truth.
Open my eyes to Your deeds,
my ears to the sound of Your call,
so that my every act
may help me share in the life of Jesus.
Give me the grace to live the example
of the love of Jesus,
which I celebrate in the Eucharist
and see in the Gospel.
Form in me the likeness of Your Son
and deepen His life within me.

To Turn from Sin

FATHER, Your love never fails.
Keep me from danger
and provide for all my needs.
Teach me to be thankful for Your gifts.
Confident in Your love,
may I be holy by sharing Your life,
and grant me forgiveness of my sins.
May Your unfailing love
turn me from sin

and keep me on the way that leads to You.
Help me to grow in Christian love.

For Faith in God's Truths

MERCIFUL Lord, hear my prayer.
May I who have received Your gift of faith
share forever in the new life of Christ.
May the continuing work of our Redeemer
bring me eternal joy.
You have freed us from the darkness
of error and sin.
Help me to believe in Your truths faithfully.
Grant that everything I do
be led by the knowledge of Your truth.
May the Eucharist give me Your grace
and bring me to a new life in You.

For the Spirit of Truth

FATHER, God of love,
guide me with Your Holy Spirit
that I may honor You,
not only with my lips,
but also with the life I lead,
and so enter Your Kingdom.
Send me Your Spirit
to teach me Your truth
and guide my actions in Your way of peace.
You are my Guide and Protector.
Grant me the grace to love You more.

For the Life of Grace

ALMIGHTY God,
my hope and my strength,

without You I fall into sin.
Help me to follow Jesus faithfully
and to live according to His Will.
Grant me a lasting respect for You
and keep me always in Your love.
Make me holy in mind and heart
and make me always eager to serve You
with all the love of my heart.
May the Body and Blood of Your Son,
which You give me in the Eucharist,
renew Your life of grace within me
that I may grow in Your love.

For God's Guidance

FATHER in heaven,
you made me Your child
and call me to walk in the light of Christ.
Free me from darkness
and keep me in the light of Your truth.
The light of Jesus
has scattered the darkness of hatred and sin.
Called to that light I ask for Your guidance.
Form my life in Your truth,
my heart in Your love.
Through the Holy Eucharist
give me the power of Your grace
that I may walk in the light of Jesus
and serve Him faithfully.

For the Joy of Forgiveness

HEAVENLY Father,
through the obedience of Jesus,

Your Son and Your Servant,
You raised a fallen world.
Free me from sin
and give me the joy of Your forgiveness.
Let sin never lead me astray.
Make me one with You always,
that my joy may be holy and true.
May Your love make me
what You have called me to be,
Your loving child and faithful servant.

To Follow Christ's Example

LORD Jesus, my Friend,
help me to be like You,
Who loved people and died for our salvation.
Inspire me by Your love,
and guide me by Your example.
Change my selfishness into self-giving;
free me from every evil
and help me to serve You with all my heart.
Keep me from my old and sinful ways
and help me to continue in the new life
of Your grace and love.
May Your Eucharist renew me
and bring me to eternal life.

An Offering of the Eucharist

GOD our Father,
Your light of truth guides us
to the way of Christ.
May I who wish to follow Him
reject what is contrary to His Gospel.

I offer You the Eucharist
to the glory of Your Name.
May it make me pure and holy
and bring me closer to eternal life.
May I never fail to praise You
for the life and salvation You give me
for the Sacrament of the Altar.

For the Peace of Christ

GOD, my Father,
from You I have my being.
Be close to me and hear my prayer.
Look upon me in my moments of need,
for You alone can give me true peace.
May I share in the peace of Christ.
Gifts without measure
flow from Your goodness to bring me peace.
My life is Your gift.
Guide my life's journey,
for only Your love makes me happy.
Keep me strong in Your love
and give me Your peace.

For Forgiveness of Sin

HEAVENLY Father, Creator of all,
may I serve You with all my heart
and know Your forgiveness in my life.
Forgive my sins and give me Your life,
Your grace and Your holiness.
Look upon me in my moments of need,
for You alone can give me true peace.
May I share in the peace of Christ

Who offered His life in the service of all.
Help me with Your kindness.
Make me strong through the Eucharist.
May I put into action the saving mystery
I celebrate in the Mass.
Protect me with Your love
and prepare me for eternal happiness.

To Serve God Well

FATHER of mercy, forgive my failings,
keep me in Your peace
and lead me in the way of salvation.
Give me strength in serving You
as a follower of Christ.
May the Eucharist bring me Your forgiveness
and give me freedom to serve You all my life.
May it help me to remain faithful
and give me the grace I need in Your service.
May it teach me the way to eternal life.

To be Cleansed from Sin

JESUS, my Redeemer,
You reward virtue and forgive the sinner.
Grant me Your forgiveness
as I come before You confessing my guilt.
May the power of Holy Mass
wash away my sins, renew my spiritual life,
and bring me to salvation.
May I never misuse Your healing gifts,
but always find in them
a source of life and salvation.
Cleanse me of sin and free me from guilt,

for my sins bring me sorrow
but Your promise of salvation brings me joy.

To Follow the Good Shepherd

MY God and Father,
give me new strength from the courage of Christ,
our Savior and Redeemer.
He is our Good Shepherd.
Let me hear the sound of His voice,
lead my steps in the path He has shown,
that I may receive His help
and enjoy the light of Your presence forever.
Strengthened by the Eucharist,
may I feel its saving power in my daily life
till I reach eternal life with You.
Lead me to join the Saints in heaven.

For Health of Mind and Body

GOD of mercy and love,
protect me from all harm.
Give me health in mind and body
to do Your work on earth.
Pour out Your Spirit upon me,
and grant me the strength of the Eucharist,
this Food from heaven,
that I may more willingly
give my life in Your service.
Work in my life with Your grace
and bring me to the joy You promise.

To be Faithful in Serving God

FATHER in heaven,
ever-living source of all that is good,
keep me faithful in serving You.
Help me to drink of Christ's truth,
and fill my heart with His love
so that I may serve You in faith and love
and reach eternal life.
In the Sacrament of the Eucharist
You give me the joy of sharing Your life.
Keep me in Your presence.
Let me never be separated from You
and help me to do Your Will.

To Grow in God's Love

LORD, my God,
increase my eagerness to do Your Will
and help me to know
the saving power of Your love.
My heart desires Your love
and my mind searches for the light
of Your Divine Word.
Give me strength
to grow in my love for Christ, my Savior,
that I may welcome the light of His truth.
Give me the grace to do good
that I may reach the Kingdom of Heaven.

For the Light of Faith

LORD Jesus, Light of the world,
fill me with the light of faith.

May that faith shine in my words and deeds.
Open my heart to receive Your life
that I may be filled with Your glory and peace.
May I share Your life completely
by living as You taught.
Make me faithful to You
that I may bring Your life to others.
Help me to live as God's child
and welcome me into Your Kingdom.

To Share the Eucharist

JESUS, my Savior,
You are my Food from heaven.
By my sharing in this mystery of the Eucharist
teach me to judge wisely the things of earth
and to love the things of heaven.
May my communion with You
teach me to love heaven.
May its promise and hope guide my way.
May it help me in my weakness
and free me from sin.
As I serve You here on earth,
strengthen me with the Bread of heaven.

For the Gift of the Holy Spirit

JESUS, Divine Word of God,
You became Man, born of the Virgin Mary.
May I come to share Your Divinity,
for You humbled Yourself
to share our human nature.
As You nourish me
with the Food of life in the Eucharist,

give me also Your Spirit,
so that I may be filled with light
at Your coming to my soul.
Lead me to rejoice in true peace.

For Eternal Life with God

HEAVENLY Father,
in glorifying Jesus
and sending us Your Spirit,
You open the way to eternal life.
May my sharing in this gift
increase my love
and make my faith grow stronger.
Send Your Spirit to cleanse my life
so that the offering of myself to You at Mass
may be pleasing to You.
May my sharing in the Eucharist,
our Bread of Life,
bring me to eternal life.

To Receive God's Spirit

FATHER of light,
from Whom every good gift comes,
send Your Spirit into my life
that I may serve You with a holy heart.
Strengthen me with Your Holy Spirit
and fill me with Your light.
Send the Spirit of Pentecost into my heart
to keep me always in Your love.
Enrich me with Your grace
so that I may praise You always
and reach eternal life.

Fulfill my hope
to see You face to face in heaven.

To Be an Offering with Jesus

LORD Jesus,
may everything I do begin with Your grace,
continue with Your help,
and be done under Your guidance.
May my sharing in the Mass
free me from my sins
and make me worthy of Your healing.
May I grow in Your love and service
and become a pleasing offering to You,
and with You to the Father.
May this mystery I celebrate
help me to reach eternal life with You.

For Growth in Faith, Hope, Love

ALMIGHTY God,
strengthen my faith, hope, and love.
May I do with a loving heart
what You ask of me
and come to share the life You promise.
Give me fidelity and love
to carry out Your commands.
Only with Your help
can I offer You fitting service and praise.
May I live the Faith I profess
and trust Your promise of eternal life.
May the power of Your love
continue its saving work in my life.

For Faith in the Risen Lord

FATHER, in Your love
You have brought me from evil to good
and from misery to happiness.
Through Your blessings
give me the help I need to continue in virtue.
Make my faith strong and my hope sure.
May I never doubt that You will fulfill
the promises You have made.
May I who am redeemed
by the suffering and death of Christ
always rejoice in His Resurrection.
As I honor His glorious Resurrection,
renew Your gift of Divine life within me.

To Be Grateful for God's Gifts

LORD Jesus Christ,
I believe in You as my God and Savior.
Make me more faithful to Your Gospel.
By sharing in the Eucharist often
may I come to live more fully
the life of grace You have given me.
Keep Your love alive in my heart
that I may become worthy of You.
Teach me to value Your gifts
and ever be grateful for them.
Help me to strive for eternal life.

To Live as a Child of God

FATHER in heaven,
when the Spirit came down upon Jesus

at His Baptism in the Jordan,
You revealed Him as Your own beloved Son.
Keep me, Your child,
born of water and the Spirit,
faithful to my calling.
May I who share in Your life
as your child through Baptism
follow in Christ's path of service to people.
Let me become one in His sacrifice
and hear His word with faith.
May I live as Your child,
following the example of Jesus.

For God's Forgiveness

MERCIFUL Father,
protect me in my fight against evil.
May the light of Your truth
give sight to the darkness of my sinful eyes;
bring me the blessing of Your forgiveness
and the gift of Your light.
Bless me, a sinner,
who asks for Your forgiveness.
Pardon my sins
and keep me faithful to Your commandments
for You do not want sinners to die
but to live with the Risen Christ.

To Share Christ's Resurrection

ALMIGHTY God,
You have given the human race Jesus Christ,
Your Son and our Savior,

as a model of humility and love.
He fulfilled Your Will by becoming Man
and gave His life on the Cross.
May His death give me hope
and strengthen my faith.
May His Resurrection give me grace
to continue in His love
and lead me to salvation.
Help me to bear witness to Jesus
by following His example in His suffering,
and make me worthy to share in His Resurrection.

For the Blessings of Holy Mass

LORD Jesus Christ,
guide me with Your unfailing love.
Protect me from what could harm me
and lead me to what will save me.
Help me always, for without You
I shall surely fail and sin.
Bring me closer to You
through prayer and Holy Communion.
May Holy Mass cleanse me from my sins,
bring me pardon and grace
and lead me to the joy of heaven.

To Be a Follower of Jesus

LORD Jesus Christ,
fill my heart with faith and love.
Fill my mind with the light of Your Gospel,
that my thoughts and actions may please You,
and my love be sincere.

Look with love upon me,
the love that You showed us
when You delivered Yourself to evil men
and suffered the agony of the Cross.
Teach me to follow Your example.
May my faith, hope, and love
turn hatred to love, conflict to peace,
and death to eternal life.

To Live a Life of Prayer

LORD Jesus,
help me to understand the meaning
of Your Death and Resurrection.
I call out for Your mercy.
Bring me back to You
and to the life You won for us
by Your Death on the Cross and Resurrection.
Help me to grow in faith and hope,
and deepen my love for You in Holy Communion.
Help me to live a life of prayer
according to Your words in the Gospel,
and seek You, Jesus, my Bread of Life,
in the Holy Eucharist.

For the Wisdom of Christ

JESUS, my Savior,
bring me back to You
and fill my mind with Your wisdom.
May my offering in the Mass,
this Sacrament of Your love,
be pleasing to You and to the Father.

Through this Sacrament
may I rejoice in Your healing power
and enjoy Your saving love in mind and body.
May I who receive this Sacrament
grow in love for the things of heaven.

For a Happy Death

MY heavenly Father,
in Your loving Son, Who rose from the dead,
our hope of resurrection dawned.
The sadness of death gives way
to the bright promise of immortality.
For Your faithful people
life is changed, not ended.
Your Son accepted death for love of You
and for the salvation of my soul.
In His Name I ask for the grace
to persevere to the end in Your love.
Keep me watchful at all times.
Keep me obedient to Your Will till death.
May I leave this world with confidence and peace
and come to share
in the gift of Christ's Resurrection.
May I be free from sin when I die
and rejoice in peace with You forever.
May I gain an eternal dwelling place in heaven.

Praise to the Holy Trinity

I PRAISE You, Father all-powerful.
I praise You, Divine Son, our Lord and Savior.

I praise You, Spirit of love.
One God, three Persons, be near me
in the temple of my soul.
Draw me to share in Your life and love.
In Your kindness grant to me
and to my family the riches of Your mercy,
and a share in Your blessings.
May we come to the glory of Your Kingdom
where we may love You for all eternity.

For God's Help in Daily Actions

OUR Father,
may everything I do
begin with Your inspiration,
continue with Your help,
and reach perfection under Your Guidance.

With Your loving care
guide me in my daily actions.
Help me to persevere with love and sincerity.

Teach me to judge wisely the things of earth
and to love the things of heaven.
Keep me in Your presence
and never let me be separated from You.

Your spirit made me Your child,
confident to call You Father.
Make Your love the foundation of my life.

Teach me to long for heaven.
May its promise and hope
guide my way on earth
till I reach eternal life with You.

For God's Blessing on Daily Work

O LORD, my God,
Creator and Ruler of the universe,
it is Your will that human beings accept
the duty of work.

May the work I do bring growth in this life
to me and those I love
and help to extend the Kingdom of Christ.
Give all persons work that draws them to You
and to each other in cheerful service.

I unite all my work
with the sacrifice of Jesus in the Mass
that it may be pleasing to You
and give You glory.

I beg Your blessing upon all my efforts.
With Saint Joseph as my example and guide,
help me to do the work You have asked
and come to the reward You have prepared.

For Priestly Vocations

O LORD, my God,
You renew the Church in every age
by raising up priests outstanding in holiness,
living witnesses of Your unchanging love.
In Your plan for our salvation
You provide shepherds for Your people.

Fill the hearts of young men
with the spirit of courage and love
that they may answer Your call generously.
Give parents the grace to encourage vocations
in their family by prayer and good example.

Raise up worthy priests for Your altars
and ardent but gentle servants of the Gospel.
Give the Church more priests
and keep them faithful in their love and service.
May many young men choose to serve You
by devoting themselves
to the service of Your people.

For a Devoted Laity in the Church

O LORD, our God,
You called your people to be Your Church.
As they gather together in Your Name,
may they love, honor, and follow Your Son
to eternal life in the Kingdom He promised.

Let their worship always be sincere,
and help them to find Your saving love
in the Church and its sacraments.

Fill with the Spirit of Christ
those whom You call to live
in the midst of the world and its concern.
Help them by their work on earth
to build up your eternal Kingdom.
May they be effective witnesses
to the truth of the Gospel
and make Your Church a living presence
in the midst of the world.

Increase the gifts You have given Your Church
that Your faithful people may continue to grow
in holiness
in imitation of Your beloved Son.

OTHER OUTSTANDING CATHOLIC BOOKS

0899423450
90000
9 780899 423456